all the best!

Ghosts of Nova Scotia

Tenth Anniversary Edition

Darryll Walsh

D1452559

Pottersfield Press, Lawrencetown Beach, Nova Scotia, Canada

Library and Archives Canada Cataloguing in Publication

Walsh, Darryll

Ghosts of Nova Scotia / Darryll Walsh. -- 10th anniversary ed.

ISBN 978-1-897426-21-0

      1. Ghosts--Nova Scotia. I. Title.

GR113.5.N69W35 2010   398.209716'05   C2010-902390-0

Cover design by Gail LeBlanc

Cover photo by iStockphoto.com

Photos by Darryll Walsh

Pottersfield Press acknowledges the financial support of the Government of Canada through the Book Publishing Industry Development Program for our publishing activities. We also acknowledge the ongoing support of the Canada Council for the Arts, which last year invested $20.1 million in writing and publishing throughout Canada. We also thank the Province of Nova Scotia for its support through the Department of Tourism, Culture and Heritage.

Pottersfield Press
83 Leslie Road
East Lawrencetown, Nova Scotia, Canada, B2Z 1P8
Website: www.pottersfieldpress.com
To order, phone toll-free 1-800-NIMBUS9 (1-800-646-2879)
Printed in Canada

For Adam …
A lost love who will haunt me
until time has no meaning.

Table of Contents

Acknowledgements

As with the first edition, this edition was only made possible with the kind and unstinting help provided to me by many people.

A great debt of gratitude is acknowledged to:

Those who gave me their time and stories during my many book signings.

Those who gave me feedback on the first edition and encouraged me to bring out another.

Peggy Amirault and Julia Swan, for their editorial assistance. Lesley Choyce, my publisher, who took a chance on an unknown author ten years ago and started me on this wonderful journey called "writing."

Valerie Innes, Sherry Yates, Mary-Anne Hopkins, Dr. Mark Goisine, and the many other people who made the first edition possible.

Introduction

Recently, someone asked me why I was writing a tenth anniversary edition of this book. A few minutes later I found out they were from out west, and it only served to accentuate differences between the Maritimes and the rest of the country. When I mention this book to Nova Scotians, their eyes light up and the excitement is palpable. Nova Scotians love their ghost stories. After politics, the weather and religion, ghosts are the favourite topic of conversation. As we learn our politics and religion from our parents and family, we develop our love of the mysterious the same way. And the mysterious unknown is not just a theoretical possibility here. It is very real to us. At every book signing people approach me and relate the stories they grew up with and still cherish today. I began collecting new stories for this edition within weeks of the publication of the original book in the fall of 2000.

Those who live on Canada's east coast are blessed with having their cultural heritage almost wholly intact. The native Mi'kmaq have been here the longest and developed a rich heritage of fantastical beliefs. Four hundred years ago they were joined by the French, English, Irish, Scottish, and German settlers, who brought with them their own vibrant folklore and beliefs. These beliefs have found fertile ground here and still capture our imaginations in a way that the busy urban centres out west do not. It's hard to be close to the past when you commute two hours a day on traffic-clogged roads through a concrete jungle, only to fight your way through dense crowds to get anything done. The pace of life here is slower, and that less hectic pace helps us to remember who we are and where we came from.

I began my initiation into the unknown as a small child. When my godparents would visit with my parents I was put to bed early to make room for adult discussions, but I stayed awake for I knew that after about an hour or so the conversation would turn to the mysterious. Those stories primed my interest. Later, the single most important influence on my life was that of my Uncle Al. He was a wonderful man, beloved by many in the small hamlet of River Bourgeois, Richmond County, Cape Breton. When I was a child, many times my parents and I would travel down to "The River" to visit Uncle Al and my grandmother, and that place is still sacred ground to me. Through a life often wracked by anxiety, loneliness and depression, The River was the one place where I could find true peace and contentment.

Uncle Al was a veteran of World War Two and had served in the Royal Canadian Air Force. Consequently, he always had plenty of books and magazines on the subject lying around and many of them found their way into my collection. His other great literary love was that of ghosts and folklore, and I would always spend the long drive back to Halifax sitting quietly in the backseat reading my latest acquisition. I didn't find out until after his death in 1998 that one of the reasons for his love of ghosts was that he, along with my mother, grew up in a house that was haunted. With the exception of the incident with the rocking chair, which I'll get to later, I was never aware of their personal experiences in that little house on the hill.

Years passed and trips to The River regrettably became rarer, especially after my grandmother died. Uncle Al and I still talked on the phone from time to time, but adulthood was calling and there were "serious" things that took precedence over the youthful dalliance with the unknown. Having a deep need to help others, I set out to become a clinical psychologist, specializing in the areas of adolescence and gay identity formation.

River Bourgeois

I made it as far as a Master's degree in counselling psychology before the inexorable pull of my past changed my future. They say you should write what you know, so I turned to writing non-fiction. Three books on the paranormal, teaching parapsychology and writing at the Nova Scotia Community College and a popular television series, *Shadow Hunter*, on the Space channel was the result. Thank you, Uncle Al.

The second most important influence on my life was the scientific training I received during my university years. It has helped me understand life and sift the nonsense from the truth in everything from politics and religion to advertising and the paranormal, just to name a few. Some say science is against the paranormal. That is incorrect. Science doesn't hate the paranormal. Science isn't against the paranormal. Science just doesn't care about the paranormal. Mostly, that is because many mysteries of the paranormal have been solved for a long time. And the rest seem too unlikely to be true. But there are some genuine unknowns still to be found in the field and there are a few scientists who seek truth in unlikely places. Personally, I am just as interested in the psychological aspects of the paranormal as I am in the paranormal itself. Why people believe and how that belief is manifested is just as fascinating to me as whether ghosts are real or not.

As a consequence, there is a duality of identity within me. Part of me is that ten-year-old boy who eagerly devoured all that he could about ghosts, and the other part is the scientist who knows there is a lot less to the paranormal than meets the eye. This becomes especially pertinent when I am writing about ghosts. Many stories are too fantastical and could have never happened the way they were described, so what should I do?

I developed a strategy that I would write about many of these stories only if they had a long history in the community or folklore of the province. In other words, I didn't choose stories that someone just made up or told to me in a bar. They have to have a respectable lineage since this book is about our haunted heritage – shared experiences of subtle horror and suspense that we carry with us our whole lives. So the story of a phantom pig with glowing red eyes made it into the book because generations of Nova Scotians grew up with that story, believed that story, and changed their behaviour accordingly.

My own personal story of suspense began in 1945. In March of that year my Uncle Augustaine was fighting in Holland and was killed in battle. It took four days for notification of this sad event to reach River Bourgeois, but my mother's family already knew about it. They didn't know which brother had died, but they knew there had been a death. For four days before the telegram arrived announcing the news, the old wooden rocking chair which sat under the side window in the kitchen had begun to rock by itself, a classic forerunner, that indicator of death. After the news arrived, it stopped and never did it again, so far as I know. When my Uncle Al died in 1998 I made sure the rocking chair came to stay with me as a personal connection with our shared past. Since then, my own "haunted" rocking chair has stayed either in the living room or my bedroom. And no, it hasn't rocked on its own.

None of this would matter very much if it wasn't for the hard work done by other writers in the field over the years. Helen Creighton's landmark opus, *Bluenose Ghosts*, has terrified and inspired many a reader for seventy years and remains the definitive bible of Nova Scotia mysteries. Other great works by Edith Mosher, Roland Sherwood, Thomas Raddall, Ted Hennigar, and William S. Crooker set the stage for the modern writer and were a welcome foundation for this book. These writers are gone now, but their work and dedication live on.

The reader will notice that I have organized the material in a unique way, beginning at the New Brunswick border and moving through the province county by county. That is because I always envision the telling of tales more as a journey into the past and into unfamiliar territory, rather than just a setting down of facts. Here you can get lost in the backwoods and byways as well as the main towns or cities. You'll encounter *bochdans*, those vengeful Gaelic hobgoblins that sometimes appear as scarecrows, and *feu follets*, the jack o'lanterns whose fiery light terrorizes those who travel after dark. Be prepared to discover fairy mounds, the underground forts of the *lutins*, and to encounter Grey Ladies, fearsome spectres who herald doom. These are just some of the ghosts that make Nova Scotia's past so rich and mysterious.

Cumberland County

Tantramar Marshes

The great Tantramar Marshes straddle the Nova Scotia/ New Brunswick border, comprising six thousand acres or eighty square miles. These flatlands with the Missiquash River flowing through them once belonged to the Acadians. The best vantage point is the old French Fort Beausejour on the New Brunswick side of the border. From there you can look across the marshes towards the rise on the Nova Scotia side two kilometres away where the old British Fort Lawrence once stood. The land between these forts was once dotted with huge barns and grazing animals but they are long gone. Still extant are the dykes built by the settlers to hold back the water, along with legends of treasure and stories of ghostly cries in the night.

When the Acadians were expelled in 1755, many had to leave behind their valuables since they couldn't take them with them. Some buried these items, planning for an eventual return. Most never did, and this treasure still remains to this day. Over the years these small caches grew into stores of great buried treasure, and there is anecdotal evidence that some people have found something of value buried throughout these marshes. Stories have been told of poor farmers suddenly coming into mon-

ey, strange signs of digging in the night and ghostly apparitions guarding hidden treasure. Practically anywhere in this area could hold a fortune just a short distance beneath your feet.

A French girl and her lover, a British soldier, came to a sad end here. They were captured by the local Mi'kmaq tribe, who were angry over the deaths of some of their young men at the hands of the British. The Mi'kmaq planned an especially torturous demise for the young lovers. When the tide was out on the Missiquash River, they tied the soldier and his lady love to stakes in the red clay that formed the banks of the river. They tied the soldier to a lower stake nearer the water, so that when the inevitable return of the tide occurred, the girl would watch her lover drown before she would meet her own end. After the waters had risen and drowned the soldier, British troops arrived to save her. But according to legend she had no desire to remain on this earth without her true love, so she lowered her head and allowed the waters to take her to join her lover in death. To this day it is said that their ghosts can be seen by the river when the tide rushes in, and if you listen carefully, the gurgling waters sound like two people drowning.

Somewhere along the river close to Fort Lawrence, there once was a road with a bridge that was the scene of bloody fighting between the British and the Mi'kmaq. It was named Bloody Bridge, but locals complained about the ghostly cries of battle and the dying that could still be heard, so the road was moved and the bridge destroyed. If you like wandering cold and lonely places, take a walk around here after you visit the fort, and you may hear the sounds of battle and the cries of the dead.

Ever since the first inhabitants came to these marshes they have reported mysterious bobbing lights moving across the land, so it is only fitting that a romantic story would be created to explain them. It is said the ghost of an Acadian girl walks the marshes with a lantern looking for her lover, who was expelled with the rest of the Acadians.

Fort Lawrence Ridge

It is never a good idea to argue with a witch. More than two hundred years ago in the late 1780s, a Loyalist named Captain Walter Tygart used to argue constantly with his neighbour, an elderly woman named Nelly Edwards. Edwards was as rough and tumble as her neighour and this, coupled with her use of natural medicines, made her seem suspicious to the God-fearing settlers of the area.

After one major argument, Tygart began to act strangely and carry both a Bible and prayer book with him wherever he went. He also began to shun the local tavern and wouldn't be seen outside his home after dark. Friends and neighbours began to worry about Captain Tygart, but soon their attention was drawn to fighting a major forest fire that threatened the whole area. It took a long time to bring the blaze under control, and many homes were lost, including that of Nelly Edwards, who perished in the conflagration. It was shortly after this that Captain Tygart was free to tell his story.

It seems Nelly Edwards used to turn him into a horse after he argued with her on the way home from the tavern each night. She would ride him in the company of three other old women on black horses to Fort Lawrence and back and with the hard riding and whipping that he received each night, Tygart became afraid to leave his house in case he would fall under Edwards' spell. The fire that killed Edwards and levelled her house set him free. It isn't known if this cured Tygart of his tempestuous ways, but it is said that if you listen carefully on a still summer's night along the ridge, you will hear the cries of Nelly Edwards echo eerily across the marshes as she burns to death.

Amherst

Coming from Amherst is one of the most documented and strangest occurrences of ghostly phenomena. Poltergeists, ghostly voices and spirit writing are all here, and they all revolved around Esther Cox in the nineteenth century.

The location of the Great Amherst Mystery was 6 Princess Street in Amherst. During 1878 and 1879 the house belonged to Daniel Teed and his wife Olive. Staying with the Teeds were their two children, Olive's brother William, Daniel's brother John, and Olive's two sisters, Jane and Esther. Esther was eighteen years old that September 4 when the first of the mysterious happenings began.

One week earlier Esther had broken up with her boyfriend, who suddenly started acted bizarrely by waving a pistol in her face and threatening her. Though shaken, Esther calmed down enough to be sleeping peacefully with her sister in the bed they shared later that night. She awoke shortly after falling asleep to the sounds of something moving under the bed. She woke Jane, they investigated and found that a box under the bed was jumping up and down as if some animal was inside. They called Daniel Teed, but when he opened the box he found nothing in it to make it act as it had. Everyone returned to bed and the rest of the night passed quietly.

The next night was interrupted by Esther screaming, "I'm dying!" When everyone rushed into the bedroom and lit some candles, they saw Esther's body was badly swollen as she cried out in pain. More sounds were coming from under the bed, but before anyone could investigate, a loud clap of thunder was heard in the room. Immediately Esther fell back to sleep and her body returned to a normal state.

From then on classic poltergeist activity began. Bedclothes were pulled off beds by unseen hands, whispers were heard, and objects moved apparently by themselves. The local doctor was called and examined Esther, but could not find anything wrong with her. It was at this time that writing appeared on her bedroom wall. "Esther Cox, you are mine to kill," was written by a ghostly hand in front of a half-dozen witnesses.

Soon knocks and raps began on the walls and ceilings. Someone began to speak to the unseen presence and it would answer questions with knocks. Naturally, the story got out and villagers flocked to the house to see for themselves the fascinating phenomena. Even the local Methodist preacher observed a pail of water start to boil when it was placed near Esther.

Esther became sick with diphtheria, and for the two-week duration of her illness no bizarre happenings occurred. She was sent to stay with relatives for a time, and upon her return she was given a new room in the house with the hope that a change of location would continue to exorcise the ghost. It was all for naught, however. Soon fires began to drop from the ceilings and after a few days of this, Esther was banned from the house.

Esther found a job and a room with a local restaurant owner, but the problem followed her there, so the poor girl was quickly returned to the Teed residence. She was then shipped off to Saint John, New Brunswick, to be studied but none of the phenomena followed her there, so she returned to Amherst. A local farmer then had the grace to offer her a place to stay and while there she lived a happy, quiet life. However, when Olive Teed intervened to have her sister returned to the Teed house, the phenomena returned with her and at an increased rate.

Walter Hubbell, an American actor and magician, then entered the picture. He stayed with Esther for five weeks and observed all that occurred around her, including knives that sped through the air at him. This gave him the idea to take Esther on the stage circuit. They arranged a show, but it flopped miserably. Not totally discouraged at this turn of events, Hubbell wrote a book on the incident called *The Great Amherst Mystery*.

Meanwhile, Esther was employed by another local farmer until his barn burnt down and she was arrested for arson. After that and until her death in 1912, Esther Cox was free of any further incidents.

Many parapsychologists have thought long and hard on this series of events, and the predominant theory is that the phenomena was triggered by the trauma of her near rape at the hands of her boyfriend the week previous to the first event. Popular opinion is that poltergeists are the product of a stressed and/or sexually frustrated mind, usually that of a female adolescent. If Esther was suffering trauma from the boyfriend incident, coupled with the theory that Daniel Teed may have been "bothering" her, then this could explain the incident using the "unconscious psychokinesis" theory of poltergeists – that the person in question is, without their conscious knowledge, moving objects through mental efforts: "mind over matter." This is, of course, deeply sexist and a product of Victorian thinking that continued into the twentieth century. There is no logical reason why a female would be any more psychically active than a male if she were stressed or sexually frustrated.

What we can be fairly certain of is that the whole episode was exaggerated. From this distance it is impossible to determine the depth of the original phenomena. But once Walter Hubbell got involved, any reports after that point are suspicious due to his shady reputation as well as his skill as a magician. He wanted to make money off Esther and the best way to do that was to exaggerate the phenomena. True paranormal phenomena are just not that exciting or dramatic.

Minudie

Amos "King" Seaman, a local merchant, landowner, businessman, and philanthropist travelled to Amherst one day in the mid-1800s on business and while there, witnessed a public hanging. The criminal was especially hated, even to the point of being refused the right of burial within the town limits. Feeling compassion for the man, Seaman brought the body back to Minudie and buried it in the local cemetery. The corpse was not destined to rest undisturbed, though, for local medical students dug it up and took the head with them to school in Boston. From that day the headless ghost of the unfortunate criminal is said to prowl the area on foggy nights looking for the scoundrels who stole his head.

Isle Haute

Almost every island in the Maritimes has some legend of buried treasure. Captain Kidd, the English privateer, is the most common culprit, but many unnamed pirates also made their temporary homes here. Unfortunately for the legends, Kidd never made it to Nova Scotia, and pirates rarely buried treasure. They preferred to spend it. But on occasion they did, as did Acadian settlers stashing family valuables before their expulsion, and wreckers after looting shipwrecks or survivors. So there are more than enough reasons to follow a treasure legend, just in case.

Isle Haute is almost perfectly situated where the Bay of Fundy turns into the Minas Channel. It is also almost halfway between French Cross Point and Cape Chignecto. The Acadians called the island Ile aux Morts, the Island of the Dead, because they believed it had the power to trap unwary ships at low tide. So it is reasonable to expect some truth to any legend of buried treasure, and indeed, there is. Legends of treasure have been associated with the island for hundreds of years, but it was only fifty years ago that concrete proof of something going on there surfaced. An American explorer, Edward Rowe, discovered

Spanish and Portuguese coins as well as a skeleton. Spanish or Portuguese ships were a rarity this far north, but we know that at least one of them made it to Isle Haute and the island may still yet have secrets to unveil.

Spencer's Island

Spencer's Island is well-known as one of the two best ship-building areas of Nova Scotia. Lunenburg serviced the Atlantic side of the province, while Spencer's Island served the Fundy Shore. It is from here that one of the most well-known mysteries began. Shipbuilding was the forte of the people there, but it is one ship in particular that Spencer's Island is famous for.

The *Amazon* was built in May 1861, a brigantine of 282 tons. Only 103 feet long, its legend dwarfs many a ship of larger dimensions. Most know the ship as the *Mary Celeste*.

In November 1872, the brigantine left New York bound for Genoa, Italy. At the same time, the British ship *Del Gratia* left New York for Gibraltar. On December 4, the *Del Gratia*, having just come out of a squall, came upon the *Mary Celeste* sailing erratically. Captain Morehouse of the *Del Gratia* became concerned and sent a boarding party over to examine the ship. However, the search party found it to be totally deserted, and no reason for its abandonment could be determined. *Mary Celeste* was in pretty good order, although there were small tears in its sails. The cargo of alcohol was still there and many valuables were untouched. A hatch was open, with some water in the hold, but nowhere near enough to have required the crew to abandon ship.

Captain Morehouse sent a crew over to the *Mary Celeste* to take her into Gibraltar. Once there, the legal niceties of salvage dragged on for some time as the theories as to what happened developed and, during the twentieth century, grew stranger.

Various theories have been put forward for the strange disappearance of Captain Briggs, his wife, their daughter and the crew of the *Mary Celeste*. Everything from the Bermuda Triangle, to UFOs, to the *Del Gratia* crew becoming pirates and seizing the ship has been proposed at one time or another. This last theory was partially to blame for the long delay in awarding the *Del Gratia* salvage money. And, as it turned out, not very much money.

The most likely explanation to the long-standing mystery is that the captain and crew became wary after some of the cargo of alcohol started leaking in the hold. Alcohol fumes are quite flammable and it was possible that the crew thought the ship was in mortal danger. They may have taken to the ship's boat and ran a line to the ship, but a squall may have developed, and the line could have been broken. A small lifeboat would not last long in the Atlantic and the captain and crew, along with his wife and daughter, would have drowned. The *Mary Celeste*, meanwhile, would have continued on its way only to be spotted by the *Del Gratia*, and the mystery was born.

Port Greville

Headless ghosts of humans are common enough, but to hear about the headless ghost of a dog is an exciting rarity. Not surprisingly, the spectral hound appears at Ghost Hollow, though not many are brave enough to hang around the hollow at night when it shows itself. The huge white hound first appeared many years ago. It appears suddenly, is impervious to any attempts to harm it, and disappears just as quickly.

Parrsboro

Parrsboro is one of my favourite towns and it has the distinction of having three haunted bridges. At Lank's Bridge, the apparition of a horse with a headless rider can be seen, apparently the result of a murder many years ago. At Frog Hollow Bridge, the ghost of a young girl can be seen and her screams can be heard, echoes of when she perished here one cold Halloween night.

A very chilling story comes from here concerning the Screeching Bridge. Every fall during the first snowfall the bridge echoes with the sounds of a woman screeching. Apparently, a woman committed suicide at the spot one year during the first snowfall of the season. She threw herself off the bridge and her last screams still terrify the residents.

Because I come from a nautical family, this next story has special interest for me. About twenty years ago a phantom freighter was seen in the harbour, apparently in trouble out by Partridge Island. Its whistle could be heard, its lights could be seen, and the freighter was just visible in the dark night. When the two witnesses left to report a ship in distress, it vanished and a search by authorities turned up nothing.

Maiden's Cave

It was 1740 and the seas were a dangerous place. Many bloodthirsty pirates sailed these waters, as well as heavily armed warships because of the continuing war between Britain and France. One ship was called *Red Hawk*, captained by Jonathan Hawkins. Captain Hawkins had taken with him his daughter Elizabeth. Usually the sea was not the best place for families, but Captain Hawkins' wife had died some years previously.

The *Red Hawk* spent an uneventful journey until they reached the Bay of Fundy. They were overtaken by the savage pirate Leonardo Deno, captain of the *Diavola*, who slaughtered all but Captain Hawkins and six of his sailors. Hawkins had thrown his daughter overboard in order to save her. After the six survivors of the crew walked the plank, Hawkins was next and the last sight he saw was that of his daughter being held by the pirates. Apparently, they had seen what he had done and had launched a boat to retrieve her.

A hurricane picked that fortunate time to come up and Elizabeth was spared for a time. The *Diavola* weathered the storm and landed near Black Point. Legend has it they saw jewels and precious stones washed ashore and filled the ship full of them.

Meanwhile, Elizabeth had spit in Deno's face and scratched him, so he decided to punish her with a cruel death. He found a cave not far from the shore and, throwing Elizabeth in it as well as some fish, he ordered it sealed.

Many years later some Mi'kmaq were investigating the area and one of them entered the cave. There he found the cave rich in amethyst and quartz, but he also found a skeleton. The story got around and some remembered hearing about the incident of the *Red Hawk*, so from this time on the cave was known as Maiden's Cave. It has been said down through the years that you can hear the anguished, ghostly cries of the girl who was sealed alive in a cave by a pirate she spurned.

Colchester County

Five Islands

It is said these five islands in Cobequid Bay were made as a result of the great Mi'kmaq god Glooscap fighting his arch-enemy, Beaver. The beaver had built a dam from Cape Split to Parrsboro and this angered the mighty Glooscap, who then threw giant handfuls of earth and stone at the dam, smashing it and letting the waters resume their natural flow. Not all of the earth and stone made it to the dam; five handfuls fell short, and these became the islands of Moose, Diamond, Long, Egg and Pinnacle.

Long Island is rumoured to be the resting place of buried treasure. Long Island is the middle island and in its centre there are three graves, with the middle one allegedly hiding Spanish doubloons underneath. A local man, Luke Leason, had gotten a pirate map from a down-on-his-luck sailor. He led a few men on a treasure hunt, but death and misadventure claimed one of them, and was in danger of claiming them all before they were rescued. Leason disappeared after that, leading some to believe he had found something, but it is unlikely that he could have taken it all away by himself. Are there still some hidden doubloons under the centre grave on Long Island? For years, it was said that a seafaring man with a leather map was seen returning again and again to the area in search of the treasure.

On Moose Island you can find a carved face of a bearded man with angry features. The angry man was John Ruff (or Buff in some accounts), and he was a mean and brutish drunkard. He abused his family until one day his son Arthur killed him. Arthur might have gotten away with it too if his younger brother hadn't squealed. Nevertheless, young Benjamin did come up with a good excuse. He claimed the Devil had taken up residence on the island and could be seen moving ghost-like around the island, just a dark shape whispering evil thoughts to those who came too near.

It turned out this excuse wasn't needed, for the boys were found not guilty since the evidence of the blow that crushed old man Ruff's skull could have also been inflicted by the accidental falling of a tree, as the boys had initially claimed.

The cliff with the angry visage of John Ruff's face is called Ruff's Ghost, and some believe the angry spirit of an angry man still walks the island. An eerie light has been seen dancing through the woods, and locals believe it is a ghostly lantern carried by the ghost of John Ruff, seeking vengeance upon the sons who have escaped his wrath. There's no word on whether the Devil ever walked on Moose Island, or if it was just the fevered imagination of young Benjamin.

Blockhouse Brook Bridge

The spectre of a murdered woman, dressed all in white, is seen eternally running from her attackers. The sounds of another poor soul are heard at Blockhouse Brook. Her spectre isn't seen, but you can hear her wailing mournfully on foggy nights.

Spidell Hill

On the top of this hill a ball of fire could be seen for many years. It was called Ross's Torch, for when it first appeared it hovered near a family farm of that name. It was a common appearance when the Ross family lived on top of the hill, but since they moved away its appearances are a rare occurrence, though reports still come in from time to time of strange unexplained lights in the vicinity.

Hants County

Shubenacadie River

The Shubenacadie River is a beautiful waterway, part of which has a three-metre tidal bore twice daily. The river runs from Shubenacadie Grand Lake just outside Halifax Regional Municipality up through Shubenacadie and Stewiacke before exiting into the Minas Basin at Maitland.

This peaceful and bucolic setting, though, has also had its dark side. Many years ago there lived a family near Shubenacadie who were known for being mean and vindictive. Pretty much shunned by most folk, the son did manage to make friends with another boy, but the friendship didn't last. Out of vindictiveness over some small slight, the son caused the drowning of his only friend.

Now, the mother of the dead boy was an evil witch and she was determined that this cruel family would suffer. They were a poor family and like many poor families they lived off the land. In this case they fished for their supper from the Shubenacadie River, which was always full of various species of fish. Once the witch went to work, though, the Shubenacadie became a dead zone. She cursed the river and swore that until the last member of that mean clan died no fish would find its way up the

Shubenacadie. The curse lasted for many years until the last remaining family member died. Now the fish have returned to the river and it is a place of peace and tranquility again.

Maitland

MacCallum House in Maitland was built by a shipbuilder in the early 1700s. It has operated as a bed and breakfast for many years and is now known officially as the Foley House Inn. It also appears to have had more than its share of guests. Local legend states Archie MacCallum murdered a slave and buried him next to the well. It is believed the restless spirit of the slave now haunts the premises, with his spectral blood appearing on the floor from time to time. Other apparitions have been seen in the windows and outside there is the woman in white who walks the shore in back of the house. And to top it all off, allegedly there was a curse put on the house and family in the 1800s by sailors who were refused succour from the inhabitants of the house. The sailors cursed the well and to this day residents refuse to drink from it.

Nearby is Lawrence House, now a provincial museum. It was the home of William Dawson Lawrence (1817-1886), a prosperous shipbuilder in the mid-1800s when the Bay of Fundy echoed with the sounds of many a ship being built. He launched his 2,459-ton *William D. Lawrence*, the largest wooden-hulled ship built in Canada, in October 1874 as a symbol of Nova Scotia's greatness.

However, besides being prosperous, William Lawrence was also a lover of fine music. Violin music was his favourite and it is said as you walk through this stately museum with many of its original furnishings, you can still hear his music. Other strange, unexplained noises are reported to come from the basement.

There is still another haunted house in the general area. Springhurst House is haunted by a knocking on various doors and a voice softly calling out "Lou."

East Noel

Bill Jessome did this story on his *Maritime Mysteries* television show and it certainly is one of the creepiest stories from anywhere in Nova Scotia. Though it only happened once, the thought it might return one day is enough to send shivers down this author's back.

In 1938, strange and terrifying sounds began to be heard through this peaceful community. Beginning early in the evening and lasting for some hours came sounds of bones knocking together. It sounded as if the dead themselves were angrily voicing their displeasure at something. I have travelled this area many times and its unspoiled beauty makes the thought of something like this hard to imagine, but late at night with fog blowing in from the Bay of Fundy, anything could be possible.

East Walton

The area around the bridge here is blessed/cursed with a wide range of eerie phenomena. The bridge itself is haunted by a woman in white, while the sounds of chains rattling come from the brook below. Mysterious lights appear along the road as a man on fire is seen dancing on the hillside. And in a vision from yesteryear, a ghostly team of horses comes trotting down the road and disappears before your eyes.

Mount Uniacke

Completed in 1815, stately Uniacke House was the home of Richard John Uniacke (1753-1830), attorney general of Nova Scotia from 1797 until his death. Now a provincial museum, Uniacke House boasts two ghosts: a mother and her daughter. The staff is unsure why Uniacke's wife and daughter have decided to remain earthbound here, but perhaps it is due to their love of this quiet estate. The ghosts of Martha Uniacke, Richard's first wife, who

died in 1803 at the age of forty, and her eldest daughter, Lady Mary Mitchell, are said to be seen walking arm in arm along the estate's lake, named for Martha, or sitting quietly inside the house. Lady Mitchell is usually at the piano and her mother sits close by watching her. Staff and visitors alike have either seen the ghostly pair or sensed their presence, so a trip to Uniacke House is well worth the time for those who either love open, quiet spaces or the exciting possibility of seeing a ghost or two.

Windsor

Windsor is the location of the home of Thomas Chandler Haliburton (1796-1865), a nineteenth-century judge and the author of the Sam Slick stories. It, too, is now a provincial museum but some say the spirit of Haliburton still calls it home. The judge's ghost is said to emerge from a secret panel in the wall of the reception hall and wander about for a while before dis-

appearing through the same section of wall. If you visit, keep a sharp eye when in the reception hall.

Also on the grounds of Haliburton House is the ghostly vision of a kilted soldier of the Black Watch Regiment, who is said to have drowned in a pond as he and his fellow soldiers marched through the forty-acre estate on their way to Annapolis from Windsor. The pond is called Piper's Pond because the unfortunate soldier was the regiment's piper. Local legend has it that if you run around the pond twenty times, the soldier will come up out of the black depths on horseback.

Also from Windsor come stories of the lonely apparition of a woman who walks along the shore of the Avon River before a storm.

Kings County

Avonport

Though the bridge here is long gone, you can still see where it once stood. As Highway 101 passes over the Gaspereau River, look to your right and you will see remnants of the old road stretching across the marshes to the abutments on either side of the river. Many years ago there was a covered bridge with a resident ghostly woman in white. She could be seen walking along the road until she disappeared inside the bridge and never came back out. Perhaps this scene was the never-ending replay of a suicide? It would be interesting to know if anyone still sees her now that the probable instrument of her self-destruction is gone.

Avonport Station

Almost everyone has heard of the famous island of mystery on the South Shore in Lunenburg County called Oak Island, but few people realize there are four Oak Islands in Nova Scotia. One is in the Medway River in Queens County, another in Fox Harbour in the Northumberland Strait and a fourth here in Kings County. I have spent many hours visiting my father's relatives and swimming here where the Avon River meets the Minas

Basin, but even I didn't know anything about this small, seemingly forgettable island.

Some believe this little Oak Island is directly connected to its bigger brother on the Atlantic side of the province. They believe that there is a natural waterway and portage route across the province with both Oak Islands guarding their respective entrances. And since one of the islands has mystery, treasure and ghosts on it, the other must be similarly endowed.

The only reference to anything mysterious that I could find pertaining to this Kings County island comes from a brief mention in Helen Creighton's *Bluenose Ghosts*. She writes that a "big bright light comes up at Oak Island and they can see the men come up as though they were hiding the treasure." A man named Joudrey lived on the island and had to move due to "unexplainable noises" when he was plowing. Nothing else has been discovered or proved beyond pure speculation, but maybe some connection to the other Oak Island only awaits investigation.

Evangeline Beach

A storm can be foretold by the appearance of a ghostly woman who walks the beach here. Not only does she foretell storms, but if she walks towards you, your life will be long. If she walks away from you, you had better start tidying up any loose ends.

Mount Denson

Both my father and grandfather worked on the railway and I have fond memories of visiting my grandfather at Windsor Junction, Mount Uniacke and other places. Both of them would have travelled through Mount Denson many times on the train as well as on the old Number 1 Highway. I'm sure they would have appreciated this story.

Over half a century ago the railway crossing at Mount Denson was the meeting place for two boys on their way to school. Sometimes one or the other would be late, and one boy, Jonny, would always whistle to his friend Gordon to wait up for him. This was a casual routine that would last for a couple of years until both boys left school to join the workforce. A few years after they went their separate ways, Jonny was killed by a train as he walked home one night along the same railway line.

There was some question as to why Jonny was on the tracks that night when he should have seen the train coming towards him and easily stepped out of danger. Some believe he had been assaulted and left on the tracks to die, though illness or suicide would have to be considered too. Witnesses seeing him shortly before his death reported him sober, so the mystery remains. Whatever the reason, Jonny died that dark night near the crossing where he would meet Gordon during their school years.

Some years later, Gordon was returning home one rainy night from a hunting trip via the railway tracks, and as he reached the crossing he heard a sharp whistle. Stopping, he wondered for a moment if it was another hunter calling to him. Then he realized he was at the same location where Jonny had been killed. This realization stayed with him as he resumed his trek home. A minute later he heard the approach of an unscheduled train which did not blow its warning horn at the railway crossing some yards behind him. Gordon jumped off the tracks, and as the train roared past he wondered if that whistle was a ghostly warning from his boyhood chum.

Wolfville

Wolfville is one of the prettier towns in the Annapolis Valley, and it is the location of Acadia University, where there is a resident ghost. In the women's residence the ghost of a blond woman haunts the Prophet's Room, a suite that was built with the residence in 1879. It is in this room that sightings have occurred of a woman calmly combing her long blond hair. No one knows the ghost's identity or why she should want to comb her hair for eternity in this room.

Cape Blomidon

It is here that Mi'kmaq legends say the great Glooscap has his home. Recently, there has been conjecture that Glooscap may actually have been Prince Henry Sinclair, Earl of Orkney from Scotland, who some believe sailed to Nova Scotia in 1395.

There are also stories of a mysterious light that can be seen flashing from Cape Blomidon, called the Eye of Glooscap. Legend states the Eye looks down upon and protects his people from harm. Local residents believe it to be light reflecting off a huge amethyst or some other treasure, and treasure hunters have spent years searching for it in vain for the light/treasure always disappears when they come close to where it should be.

Kentville

A local inn here boasts the ghost of an artist. The artist hanged himself because of a woman and since then, there have been strange noises, and in one instance, he appeared and crawled in bed with a guest.

The northeastern end of Kentville is known as Mocassin Hollow in official books, but the locals who know its tragic history have a more sinister name for it. In 1747, before the final acquisition of Nova Scotia by the British, soldiers of the Empire clashed with French soldiers, Mi'kmaq and some local men, resulting in many deaths. Since that time the spectres of the unfortunate dead are said to roam this area, disturbing local residents, and giving a new name, Bloody Hollow, to this sad, yet beautiful place.

Though there is no possibility of Bigfoot existing in the Maritimes, some of the stories can be quite thrilling nonetheless. This one came from one of my students whose best friend was posted to Camp Aldershot in the mid-1980s.

The best friend was present one summer night when two military policemen came in from their perimeter patrol, shaken and restless. Apparently, they were driving around the perimeter of the camp in an open jeep when on the back road they were assailed by a sudden, overwhelming stink, like garbage that had lain out in the hot sun too long. Gagging, they stopped the jeep and before they could look for the source of the smell, something bulky, tall and shaggy walked across the road about twenty feet in front of them. Needless to say, they declined to follow it and the patrol was over. After the MPs calmed down and resumed their patrol, there was no further sign of the creature and no further incidents.

A couple of years previously one of my researchers had been in the area in the late spring or early summer when he smelled this sickening odour of garbage accompanied by a sudden, intense bad feeling. He immediately left the area, but was aware that something in the trees was following him, always keeping out of sight. He naturally thought it was a bear or coyote, but later when he heard the story of the MPs, he wondered if the incidents were related.

Berwick

Another possible Bigfoot sighting occurred in April 1969, when there were reports of an eighteen-foot creature roaming outside the town. Described as very tall and dark, it was seen running across a field at about twenty miles per hour. Nicknamed The Phantom, it caused such interest that the local police had quite the traffic control problem for a few days. Whatever it might have been, reports ended after a few days and nothing has been heard of it since.

Hall's Harbour

During the War of 1812, pirates would often put in to small harbours for provisions, for safety, or for companionship. In 1813, Captain Samuel Hall was making a fair booty plundering the American coast. He was also in the habit of plundering a small village nine miles from Kentville. The settlers of this town didn't take very kindly to this, and on May 30 of that year they planned to ambush the captain. It only partly worked, and Captain Hall managed to get away. However, he lost his treasure when the settlers ambushed a member of his crew who was attempting to hide it. The blood of the now dead pirate scared the settlers and they buried the treasure themselves. Superstition kept them away from the site for some time and eventually they forgot the final resting place of the fortune. Not surprisingly, the lure of Captain Hall's lost treasure has led many a brave soul to search along the shores of this picturesque harbour. It is said that when the treasure seekers begin to dig down looking for the loot, sounds of oars are heard from across the water and six burly men and youths rise up out of the water to stand watch over the stash.

Also seen at Hall's Harbour are the ghostly lights of a ship sailing up the Bay of Fundy every seven years. It makes no sound, no crew can be seen on deck, and no one knows the reason for its appearance. It may be related to Captain Hall's treasure or it could be one of many ships that met their doom in these waters over the years.

And finally, each fall, late in the day, the lights of a ghost car can be seen travelling down the road leading to the harbour. The appearance of the car is said to be related to the death of a pedestrian who was struck and killed on this road, and buried in a nearby pasture.

French Cross Point

This ancient Acadian settlement played a role in the escape of some Acadian settlers during the Expulsion of 1755. They hid in the surrounding hills with the help of the Mi'kmaq, and waited for things to settle down. In time many died due to sickness or old age and the French Cross Burying Ground was established to house the dead. A large wooden cross was erected at the graveyard, the only sign remaining of a desperate flight. Eventually, the settlers escaped, leaving from what is now French Cross Point. The Acadians were rumoured to have left most of their valuables behind, taking only what they could carry easily, hoping to return to recover the rest later. Most never did, but treasure hunters through the centuries have looked for these fabled riches at French Cross Point.

Unlike many other treasure sites, this old burial ground is protected by a ghastly spectre. Treasure hunters have reported being chased from the graveyard and surrounding areas by a long, yellow spirit. Those who managed to dig without molestation from the spirit report the treasure always falls away deeper into the dirt when they are just about to reach it. Not many treasure seekers venture near anymore, viewing the place as cursed and seeking their fortune elsewhere.

Annapolis County

Margaretsville

From here comes the story of the mysterious silent lady. She suddenly appeared one summer evening walking up from the beach. One couple watched as she walked up their path and came right into their house without knocking on the door. She sat at the kitchen table, saying nothing, but since she was very well-dressed, the couple were polite and tried to engage her in conversation. She would say nothing, though, even when asked her name. The family stayed with her all night, but she remained mute. The next morning she got up from the chair she spent the previous twelve hours on and walked off as silently as she had come, never to return. Nothing could be learned from the many fishermen or shipbuilders along the shore, so thoughts soon turned to the supernatural. With the preponderance of ghostly women in white or grey along the Annapolis Valley, this was quite natural. If the silent lady of Margaretsville ever appeared to any other family in the neighbourhood, it was never recorded.

Bridgetown

Just after you leave Bridgetown on the way to Annapolis Royal you will cross a small bridge that spans a tributary of the Annapolis River. The bridge is nestled between two hills, and the creek it spans is popularly called Bloody Creek, for 250 years ago a massacre of British troops took place at this spot by Acadian Irregulars. It is said that the waters still run red with spilled blood on the anniversary of the battle.

Annapolis Royal

Little is left of the once major fortress of Fort Anne, which protected this former capital of Nova Scotia. Still, enough remains on these placid grounds to give the visitor a taste of its former glory. Ironically, one of the newer buildings built in the twentieth century houses the ghost. The caretaker's house is filled with strange sounds of people walking in the attic, soft music playing in the night, and unease felt by those who go down to the basement. Something or someone from a more glorious past must still walk the night here.

In the oldest house of the town there is a set of ghosts that appear from time to time. The Checkered Lady is the most famous. She appears in the rocking chair that she died in, wearing the same dress. In the house as well is the ghost of a slave girl who met her end locked up alone in a closet.

Also coming from Annapolis Royal is the story of a ghostly duel. Legend has it that a suitor of a lovely local lady was late one day in meeting his true love. When he finally arrived at her residence, he told a surprising story to her and her family. Apparently, the night before he stayed at a local inn that is now the location of the Royal Bank. During the night he was awoken by the sounds of someone trying to get into his room. When he got himself half out of the covers, he was frightened by the appearance of two men dressed in clothes from long ago. To add to his fright, the men were armed with long sabres and proceeded to have a duel in his room. The duel finally ended when one of the men ran the less fortunate one through and then tossed him out the window. Upon this act, the victor winked at the frightened guest.

The sight of the ghostly duel scared the guest so badly that he was too frightened to move for quite some time and this accounted for his lateness at his lady love's place. The woman and her family did not really believe him, yet years later when the inn was torn down so the present Royal Bank could be built, a skeleton was found buried below with a sabre alongside him. There is no word on whether the ghostly phenomenon has maintained itself in the new building.

In the marshes outside of town a ball of fire can be seen floating over the ground. They call it a banshee, but it doesn't resemble the typical Irish Banshee that wails to foretell a death.

Granville Ferry

Many years ago a young girl was thrown from a wagon and killed. She had been a common sight driving her horses and wagon along the roads around here. For some reason, every seven years you can hear the horses and wagon clattering along the road. The ground shakes and a warm breeze blows up as if caused by the passing of this invisible wagon.

Also at Granville Ferry, in an old Victorian house named The Moorings, the ghost of a former owner still walks her house. The house had been owned at one time by a kindly elderly lady, well respected by those in the community. Her spirit is not a problem most of the time. She seems to be most active whenever there are major renovations made to the house.

Port Royal

The Habitation is a wonderful reconstruction of the first major French settlement in Canada. Many schoolchildren are taken to it yearly to experience the authentic atmosphere of those first settlers. I myself have pleasant memories of my grade seven class trip late in June, just before summer vacation. There are many old stories of treasure being either buried at Port Royal or removed from the Habitation and buried nearby. One of the stories states treasure was stashed in the old foundations of the Habitation and this has led many a curious visitor to wonder if it may still be there, somewhere under the new edifice.

Stoney Beach

The headless Grey Lady of Stoney Beach walks the shore here, eternally waiting for someone to ask her real name and the name of her murderer. Legend has it she was the mistress of a fisherman from the Annapolis Basin who had a wife and family at home but brought this young woman with him on his voyages. After a while, tiring of the situation and not knowing what to do with her, he brought her ashore in a rowboat and killed her by cutting off her head. Now she walks the shore where she died, dressed in the drab grey outfit of her last day on earth, waiting for you to ask her the name of her murderer.

Helen Creighton was never sure whether there was more than one Grey Lady or if this wraith moved around a lot. Not only has she been seen here at Stoney Beach, but reports of her dressed in a long grey cloak and bonnet have come from many parts between Digby and Upper Granville. On the road, deep within salt marshes, and along the sea strand she has been sighted in these areas. There is even a tragic postscript to this story. One day many years ago a young man thought it would be funny to dress up like the Grey Lady and scare some picnickers. He did so and was shot and killed.

Nearby, along the road from Stoney Beach to Delaps Cove come the pitiful cries of a murdered peddler who calls out, "Don't kill me!"

Thorne's Cove

Between Stoney Beach and Victoria Beach at Thorne's Cove there is another spectre of a peddler who jumps out of the bushes along the road and frightens travellers. Also from here come reports of sounds of a horse and wagon which can only be heard and never seen. The sound begins down at the water's edge, and then travels towards Victoria Beach before going off the side of the road and fading away.

Port Wade

Not much is known about this spectre, but it is unusual so it is included in our eerie collection. There is a bridge here at Port Wade that has a strange reputation. It is said a phantom pig with fiery eyes appears by the bridge on cold dark nights.

Victoria Beach

Along the cliffs here you can see the ghost of a woman who committed suicide. Unlike most of our wandering ghost women, this one can clearly be seen wearing an apron. Nearby a pall cloth, the fabric laid across the face of a newly deceased person, can be seen blowing across the road. For those brave enough to follow it, treasure awaits them.

A sea serpent can be seen from the beach from time to time. Reports put its length between forty and eighty feet, and it is dark in colour with a horse-like head. Once it even followed a ship for sixty miles before giving up the chase.

There are two hills here that have resident phantoms. Parr's Hill is haunted by the apparition of a big black dog and at Andrew's Hill another dog appears, but only every seven years. You can also hear the phantom dog's chain rattling, which serves as a warning for some to beat a quick retreat.

Milford

From Milford comes the story of the Ingram Carriage House. This house used to be an inn at one time, and legend has it that suspicious things went on there during its heyday. Rumours of guests being murdered for their valuables swirled around the inn while it was in operation. It is now supposed to be haunted by a couple of "different" spectres. First, there is the ghost that is seen walking down the stairs, and second, there is the ghost of a female that is seen upstairs in a nightgown. The interesting thing about these two apparitions is that people only see half of them! My contact wasn't sure which half of them is seen, but if they conform to most ghosts, then it would have been the bottom half that was missing.

Usually, if you see a ghost and its legs or feet are missing, it means the floor of the dwelling has been raised at some time. The typical ghost walks along at the correct plane for "their" time. If there have been any changes to the structure since then, a ghost will not notice. That is why they are seen to go through walls, for if there was a door there in the past, it will still be there for the ghost.

Lequille

There is yet another buried treasure legend from around these parts. According to this legend, a group of soldiers left Port Royal and took a large amount of gold with them. However, this was a time of uncertainty with raids from New England being common and British encroachment getting closer. For safekeeping the soldiers decided to bury the treasure somewhere along the Lequille River, determined to retrieve it when the situation was safer. No one knows if they ever returned to get their gold.

Digby County

Sandy Cove

From Sandy Cove comes the strange story of a man who was abandoned here 150 years ago. In 1864, a foreign ship was spotted off the Digby Neck shore. Local residents had never seen a ship like it before and the next morning they found a man with his legs amputated below the knees lying on the beach. The operation performed on his legs looked to be professionally done and of recent origin. No information was forthcoming from the victim, however, for he refused to speak, except for a word that sounded like Jerome, so that was the name he was given.

Jerome was well-dressed in the best clothes, but any identifying marks had been removed. He was assumed to be of European royalty, and his apparent understanding of English, French, Italian, and other languages seemed to bear this out. Once he was caught off guard when asked where he came from and answered, "Trieste." Another time he surprised those taking care of him by giving them the name of his ship, *Colombo*. Unfortunately, no one seems to have followed up this lead and in the forty-eight years of his life spent here, Jerome gave no further clues as to his identity.

There was an incident that only added more mystery to the story. He had a visit from two women, who took him into another room away from the family and conversed in an unknown language for a time. This only seemed to add to the rumours that he was of noble birth and that these women were sent to make sure he was well in his exile. After this, no further clues were ever given as to his identity. He died as he arrived, in silence, in 1912.

However, due to the diligent research of Justice Savary in the 1930s, the mystery was solved. (This fact is usually glossed over by many writers. For an excellent read on the Jerome story, look for Fraser Mooney Jr.'s *Jerome: Solving the Mystery of Nova Scotia's Silent Castaway*, 2008.) Jerome's real name was Gamby and he was dropped off on our shores by a ship from New Brunswick. He had lost his legs in an accident and was taken care of by the people of Chipman, New Brunswick, until his misogyny and drain on the coffers of the town got to the point where he had to go. And thus a mystery was born.

Tiverton

Many years ago lived a man named Bramber who had an evil reputation. Many locals made the comment that if anyone would go to hell when they passed on, it would be Bramber. One stormy night, when he was very old, Bramber left his house and disappeared. The old man always left his shoes on the porch outside, preferring to walk barefoot in the house, and would stop to put them on before he left each day. Wherever he went, and with whomever he met that dark night, apparently he didn't need his shoes. People around Tiverton were sure the Devil wouldn't stand on formalities and bare feet would be most acceptable for where Bramber was heading.

Fairies/Lutins in Digby County

Fairies are most often connected with Irish or Scottish folklore, so it comes as a surprise to some to learn the Acadians also have strong fairy lore. To them, they are called *lutins*, and like the Celtic fairies, *lutins* are just as mischievous or dangerous. Most people associate fairies with Tinkerbell. The truth is far different. I suggest the documentary *Fairy Folio* by Frank Forestall for those who want to experience the whole dimension of fairies.

Residents throughout the county have reported unusual phenomena usually connected with *lutins*. Near sunset, strange noises like the flapping of wings of a large flock of birds flying unseen overhead are heard. Dogs bark at unseen things and bells toll for no reason. Ghostly sounds of beautiful singing or invisible vehicles driving past homesteads are common.

Yarmouth County

Carleton

There are at least a couple of resident apparitions in Carleton. From the area known as Clovelly Farm, you can see the ghost of Nathalie, an Acadian girl who attempted to flee the expulsion and was killed. Also, on June 24, St. Jean Baptiste Day, the figure of a Mi'kmaq man and his footprints can be seen by the Carleton River.

On Clovelly Farm you can also find five oak trees that have grown together over the years to form a single tree. A space in the middle has filled with water and never goes dry. In fact, it overflows and this is attributed to a Mi'kmaq boy who planted the tree as a symbol of his faith and optimism. The water is even believed to have blessed properties and to work miracles.

Darling Lake

There is a charming inn here called Churchill Mansion for those who seek beautiful and atmospheric accommodations of an earlier time.

Churchill Mansion got its name from Aaron Churchill, a businessman who made his name in the cotton trade as well as the slavery trade. Churchill mostly spent his time in Savannah, Georgia, but summered here with his two nieces, one of whom, it was said, he had an inappropriate relationship with. It is this niece, Lottie, who reportedly still haunts the inn. In fact, if her picture is moved from its usual place in the hall to any other room or wall, business drops off sharply until it is returned.

Unwary sleepers report a feeling of someone sitting on the bed. One woman ran downstairs to announce that as soon as she switched off the light she felt someone crawl into bed with her and begin to lie on top of her. On another occasion a staff member thought she misplaced her key to her room and spent a long time searching for it with no success. Upon returning later that day with the spare key from the manager, she was amazed to find her key lying on top of her pillow as if gently placed there by the ghost. When she checked with the other staff and manager, she learned no one had returned her key or been in her room.

After Aaron Churchill died of natural causes in 1920, the house went to his niece Lottie, but she was not to be happy. Her husband was murdered and Lottie began to go insane. She was first committed to McLeans Hospital in Boston before a place was built for her at Cape Cod, where she was to spend the last thirty years of her life. But some part of her ever more disorganized mind must have remembered Churchill Mansion, for it is believed she has returned here for eternity.

Also from Darling Lake comes the story of The Lady of the Lake. For many years there have been stories of a woman with long, white hair and wearing a long, white dress standing in the middle of a nearby road or on the shore, looking out over the lake.

Tusket

Just off the Number 3 Highway as it curves around an inlet stands a large, crooked oak tree that has an eerie history. Apparently, in the early days of settlement lynching was common and this gnarled, crooked tree was the preferred instrument for the hangings. Soon, even legally condemned criminals were hanged from this oak tree and it served its gruesome purpose for many years. When the road was upgraded sometime later, it had to go around this tree for workers couldn't cut it down. Axes wouldn't harm it and teams of oxen couldn't pull it out of the ground.

Yarmouth

From Yarmouth comes the story of Rub-A-Dub. It concerns an old inn called Vengeance House, named after a British warship and a popular watering hole in its time. But in 1807, Vengeance House became known for something else. A young girl named Mary Smith was the first to experience the phenomenon of a force that would knock on the head of her bed. In time it would knock on the walls, under her feet, and in response to questions. Many researchers investigated this phenomenon, but no one could explain it. Eventually, Mary Smith died and the inn was torn down. I have not heard if any strange phenomenon has occurred at the new house.

Two hundred years ago the brigantine *Yarmouth* was built in and launched from this town on the tip of the province. On its maiden voyage to the West Indies the brig disappeared and was declared lost at sea. Two years later in 1812, the ship was finally sighted coming into the harbour one dark, still night. Even though it was a calm night, *Yarmouth* sailed silently at full speed into the harbour before suddenly stopping just short of the wharf. It dropped anchor, and a crowd began to gather excitedly, still believing nothing was amiss except for her tardy return.

Suddenly a storm blew up and thick black fog settled over the harbour. The *Yarmouth* couldn't be seen at its anchorage so the onlookers had to wait for first light. At dawn all were amazed to find it gone. The vessel had vanished in the dark stormy night. Or its ghost certainly did. For years afterwards on the anniversary of its expected date of arrival, the spectral brigantine would replay its ghostly return home.

For 140 years the Yarmouth County Jail was the temporary home of some of Yarmouth's not-so-finest. Though it is now vacant, awaiting a decision on its future, it is not alone in its wait. Strange noises and hammerings, often accompanied by wild temperature swings, are reported. Articles are moved around even when no one is near. The apparition of a woman has been seen endlessly walking the halls and the sounds of her footsteps echo throughout the building.

She has some company, though. A man can be heard crying out in agony and the smell of burning flesh turns the stomachs of the observers. Local folklore believes that the man was somehow burned alive in his cell, probably purposely. For that man, the hell of the Yarmouth County Jail lives on.

Overlooking Yarmouth Harbour on Main Street is the Captain's House. It was built in the early 1800s and eventually owned by Captain Jacob Hatfield, who had a melancholy wife named Eleanor Jane. Eleanor, nicknamed Gramma Jake for obscure reasons lost to history, never got over the trauma of one of her sons leaving home to sail the seas like his father. Eventually, her husband died and her grief was too much to bear. Most say she fell from the widow's walk on top of the house, though some believe she simply passed away in her sleep one night. Regardless of how she died, it is said she still remains at the house, clad in white or grey and silently walking through it. Mysterious unexplained lights have also been seen dancing around the widow's walk, sometimes accompanied by the mournful lament of a ghostly set of bagpipes.

Murder Island

Of all the names in Nova Scotia this one has to be one of the strangest and most unsettling. And it has some unsettling stories to go along with its name.

It was in the 1700s that the stories began. It was said that human skulls could be seen lying on the beach, bleached white by the sun and sea. During the 1800s there were said to be hundreds of bodies lying on the beach. Various theories were advanced for these sightings. Some claimed the skulls or bodies were from clashes between settlers and the Mi'kmaq, or perhaps sick people from passing ships were let off to die on the lonely shore.

Oak Island was also mentioned, the popular theory being that the workers drafted to dig the tunnels on Oak Island would have been killed in order to protect the momentous secret. According to this theory, Murder Island is where the workers were executed and their bodies left for the birds and bugs to feast upon.

Whatever the correct theory, Murder Island's grisly past haunts it still.

Eastern Money Island

This island on the Tusket River gets its name from the beliefs of the first settlers that pirates would bury their treasure upon its shores. Since that time, many searchers have combed the shores and interior for signs of the "untold riches" that await them. Locals believe that Guardian Spirits protect the treasure and all attempts at finding it will fail. Thus far they have been correct since no one has been lucky enough to find anything of substance on the island.

Shelburne County

Mud Island

On December 18, 1883, a vicious storm hit the area and *Amaranth*, a brig bound for New York, anchored here. Five sailors and a woman were swept overboard during the storm, their bodies lost for days. They were buried and forgotten until years later when excavations were being carried out and workmen suddenly happened upon a grisly find. All that remained of the five sailors were their bones. But the most startling find concerned the remains of the woman who also lost her life that stormy day. Her body was as white as marble and very lifelike. She apparently turned to stone and was referred to as the Petrified Woman. This curiosity drew quite a few crowds until the residents of the island reburied her in a secret grave so that she – and they – could get some peace.

Cape Sable Island

In 1976, stories began to emerge about an enormous sea serpent seen off the coast. The creature was described as having two tusks that hung down from its upper jaw. It also had large, red saucer-like eyes, and was estimated to be between forty and fifty feet, grey in colour, and heavily barnacled. Its tail was described as being fish-like, not whale-like. This terrifying monster was only seen for a few days, but its brethren have been spied off our coasts for centuries.

In the middle of the island are the Centreville Woods. There is a big rock here called the Ghost Rock, named for the resident spirit. This apparition is a young woman with a long white gown who is seen crossing the road nearby. No one knows who she is supposed to be or has been brave enough to ask her personally.

Nearby, on the south side of the island in the middle of the night a mysterious light appears and floats along the beach, sometimes following unwary observers.

Shag Harbour

From Shag Harbour comes one of ufology's greatest mysteries, and one that is sure to only grow in importance like the alleged crash of a UFO reported in Roswell, New Mexico, in 1947.

Shortly after eleven p.m. on October 4, 1967, a large unidentified object with amber-coloured lights was seen descending towards Shag Harbour. Witnesses believed the object was about to plunge into the water, but it was seen to float on the sea about a thousand feet from the shore, apparently drifting with the tide.

The witnesses notified the local Royal Canadian Mounted Police detachment, which sent two cruisers to the area to investigate. The object was estimated to be sixty feet wide and about ten feet high with a single pale yellow light noticeable. The RCMP and original witnesses believed the craft to be a downed plane and were now concerned with any possible survivors. But before they could notify Search and Rescue (SAR) in Halifax, or respond with local boats, the object slipped beneath the waves. When the police and several fishermen did set out for the last known location of the "craft" they were surprised to find a half-mile-long foamy trail floating on the water about a mile offshore.

The search for "survivors" from the downed "plane" came up empty, and about an hour later a Canadian Coast Guard cutter came on the scene. About this time, SAR Halifax reported that all commercial, military and private aircraft were accounted for all the way along the eastern seaboard.

The search then officially ended, but many questions remained. The official RCMP documents and reports referred to the object as a UFO, and the Royal Canadian Air Force also called it a crashed UFO. In the following year, the Condon Report on UFOs referred to this crash as Case #34 and classified it as unsolved after looking at all other possible explanations, such as meteors and crashed space hardware.

Yet 1967 wasn't the first time a mystery light appeared at Shag Harbour. For many years, there have been reports that before a storm, balls of light dance through the air, often in a figure-eight pattern.

Shag Harbour is known for more than just UFOs, though. Residents have a ghostly remnant of European lore. For centuries people have feared the corpses of suicides. For religious reasons, bodies of suicides could not be buried in consecrated ground. It was decided to bury them at a crossroads where the unhappy spirit of the suicide would be confused about where to go once it "woke up." To forestall even this, many times a stake would be driven through the corpse's heart to "lay" the ghost.

Such is what happened here at Shag Harbour in the mid-1800s. An unhappy man by the name of John "Twinkie" Nickerson committed suicide and was buried at a local crossroads with a stake through his heart. To this day the area is called Twinkie's Corner and only the brave would tempt the folk remedy by lingering around the corner on dark and foggy nights.

Cape Negro

Stories are told here of a fully rigged sailing ship, ablaze in light, with no one on board, sailing the local waters. Unlike many ghost ship legends, no one knows the identity of the ship or the reason for its appearance. Also seen late in the evening, just before dark, is the phantom of a devil hound that comes up out of the brook and scares travellers crossing the bridge.

In addition, a ghost light comes out of the water before a storm here, apparently connected to the unfortunate deaths of two boys who died one day while out hunting. As the light comes out of the water it is small, but then begins to grow until sometimes observers can see a figure inside like a man swinging a lantern. The light has been seen along the shore, out upon the water and floating through the meadows. Without fail, the next day brings a storm to rattle the house.

Port Saxon

The old bridge at Port Saxon has had some strange stories associated with it over the years. In its early years the bridge was a covered one and a phantom horse and carriage could be heard rushing through the dark as if the hounds of hell were chasing it. But before it could emerge in front of terrified onlookers, all would go silent and the phantoms would disappear. At another time, a respected reverend saw a headless woman throw herself from the bridge. Another common occurrence was that of a wandering woman in white who led a parade of white geese across the highway nearby.

Shelburne

From Shelburne comes the story of a poltergeist that haunted the Gill family throughout the early 1970s. It mostly consisted of strange noises and the sound of things being moved, with no evidence of such. It became more pronounced when the children were left alone, as is the case with most poltergeists, because children tend to let their imaginations run wild.

The Bear's Den Bed and Breakfast on Water Street sometimes has mysterious knocks, ringing doorbells, and cold drafts when no one is around to cause them.

Also from Shelburne Harbour comes part two of the 1967 Shag Harbour Incident. Apparently, the object that crashed-landed at Shag Harbour moved underwater up the coast to the outer reaches of Shelburne Harbour. At that location was a supersecret submarine location and tracking station. Needless to say, this alerted high officials in the Canadian and American governments.

Soon military units from both countries showed up at Shelburne. American and Canadian navy ships were offshore, and dive teams were sent to the bottom to investigate this foreign/alien object. All this activity got the Soviets interested and soon Soviet subs were in the area and had to be shooed away.

Although many of the people involved are reluctant to speak, some details have come to light. It seems there were two objects in the area, one "helping" the other. The objects were not believed to be Soviet or other Communist Bloc vessels. Rumours circulated that the objects were tracked for seven days as they moved towards the Maine coast and then disappeared. There is the possibility that this was some secret "black" operation of one of the American intelligence organizations, or connected with Soviet incursions in regards to the super secret Canadian military surveillance post to track Russian submarines located nearby. Of course, ufologists believe the incident was that of a crashed alien spacecraft, but other than stories relayed by those who claimed they were there at the time, there is no hard evidence to back up this exciting, if unlikely, possibility.

Mystic Farm

Running between the 103 and Number 3 Highways outside of Shelburne is the Jordan Branch Road. From here comes the story of an elderly ghost named Nina, who haunts a picturesque place called Mystic Farm. Nina is a former owner of Mystic Farm, and she has decided to stay around and keep looking after the old homestead she loved so well.

The present owners of Mystic Farm know when Nina is around, for she announces her presence with the traditional cold spot or smell of smoke. On occasion, the owners even catch sight of Nina making her rounds, and they have become quite used to her. The second ghost, however, is another matter.

Whereas Nina is content to go about her business quietly, the second ghost makes its presence known by incessantly knocking on the back door. It is believed this ghost is that of a young man who died in a car accident nearby, and whose spirit is seeking assistance from beyond the grave.

Clam Island

It is a popular belief that ghosts cannot cross water and this next story would seem to bear that supposition out. One afternoon a man was rowing his boat home and passed close to Clam Island. He heard a shout and standing on the shore was a man he had never seen before asking to please take him off the island. Not trusting the stranger, the sailor kept going but the man called to him again, and again the sailor ignored him. The stranger kept walking along the shore following the progress of the boat and pleading to be taken off. Finally, he revealed himself to be a ghost by saying, "Do you mean to say that I have to stay here for another hundred years?" Needless to say, the sailor made it home in record time that day.

On another occasion, some men travelled to the island to do a little treasure hunting. They knew where to dig and after a while and much sweat the man in the hole suddenly froze when he saw something he couldn't describe. It left him paralyzed for a time and he had to be helped off the island by his comrades. There is no word on what it was that so terrified him or whether they were brave enough to resume searching another time.

Queens County

White Point Beach

Stories have come to me of ghostly footsteps walking across the dining room and entering the kitchen. The footsteps may be related to the spectre that haunts the grounds of the resort. A caretaker named Danny was a long-time employee of this popular holiday destination and many people believe he is still around keeping an eye on things.

Another ghost is seen on one of the islands nearby. The apparition is that of a preteen boy wearing coveralls who stands on the rocks, sometimes waving to those on shore. It is believed the boy was the young son of the West family, who lived in the area in the 1920s and who had a camp on one of the islands. One day he went out on a raft and never returned, but it appears his ghost has come back many times.

Liverpool

In my first *Ghosts of Nova Scotia*, I was disappointed by the lack of stories I had for this area. I was pleased, therefore, to see my colleague, Vernon Oickle, had collected many for his books on ghosts in the Maritimes.

One of my best friends is from Liverpool, so I travel there at least once a year and always look for the location of one or more of the stories I have heard. The swamp near Birch Avenue is one of those places. Birch Avenue is a short dead-end street with little traffic, but the exciting action occurs in the swamp. The spectre of a man in a black overcoat can be seen crossing the rotting wooden bridge that spans the swamp. Once across, the man disappears under the bridge, only to reappear some minutes later, this time as a spectral dog. Though no one can be certain, popular belief is that the two ghosts are one and the same, and this would be a rarity in a haunting since ghosts typically retain an image forever.

Outside of Liverpool was once a haunted swamp that has since been filled in and a house built over it. Normally I do not include imprecise locations, but this story is one of a rare breed. It concerns a sight straight out of Washington Irving's story *The Legend of Sleepy Hollow* and the movie based on it, *Sleepy Hollow*, starring Johnny Depp.

Many years ago a man on a horse was evading local authorities and decided to try a risky escape by crossing this swamp. They rode in at full gallop, but were never seen to ride out again. Some believed the man escaped and relocated to another town, but most people believed he and his horse perished in the swamp. Shortly after this, locals began reporting stories of a headless ghost rider and horse coming out of the swamp. It is interesting that the ghost rider appears headless. After all, his body was intact when he went into the swamp.

Liverpool has a well-deserved reputation for haunted taverns. Both Dexter's Tavern and the old West Tavern have a long history of mysterious phenomena. They were owned by sisters and opened in the mid-1700s.

Dexter's Tavern, which was located on Main Street close to Fort Point, was built in 1763 just as the large migration of New England Planters began to wind down. As the name suggests, it was originally used as a tavern and inn, although now it is a private residence.

The house was built using trees from the area, but the basement was built with large, heavy stones that some believe came from Louisbourg after it was taken by the English. Perhaps this explains the presence of the ghost. Although it is heard more than seen, when visible the ghost is that of a small man in uniform who walks back and forth in the master bedroom. Some believe his spirit was brought here from Cape Breton with the foundation stones, while others believe he is the spirit of a soldier who spent many a good time at the tavern. A chill will sometimes precede his appearance, and he has been known to open locked doors and cause knocking sounds from time to time.

He seems a friendly presence and causes no fear in the residents of the house. Locals say the phantom walks around the tavern as if guarding it for eternity. (I am especially grateful to Carol Matthews-Horsley for allowing me access to her original 1973 report on Dexter's Tavern.)

Like the Dexter Tavern, the West Tavern is also located on Main Street and is now a private residence, named the Chandler House. Ghostly footsteps in broad daylight are the primary manifestation of this phantom. Like the soldier spirit of Dexter's Tavern, this spectre seems to be on guard too. It sounds like he is walking up stairs and across the upper landing of Chandler House with a heavy step that is akin to a soldier's walk. No one has ever seen this soldier, but the inhabitants always feel his presence.

Many charming inns boast now of their "spirited" atmospheres and Lane's Privateer Inn is no exception. This inn has the added benefit of being built on ground that once was used for public hangings.

Lane's Privateer Inn is an old building that has undergone many renovations through the years. Most of the mysterious happenings occur on the third floor, particularly room 134. No one has an explanation for why this room is so special, but the room's door likes to open and close by itself, things move around the room and the feeling of an unhappy presence is felt there. Below, a male figure sits at the end of the bar, but when the bartender goes to wait upon him, he is gone. A popular trick of the ghost is to walk through the inn's front door then disappear.

Sandy Cove

Tan Brook in Sandy Cove is haunted by the apparition of a calf with luminous eyes like balls of fire. There was also a sighting of a mysterious man who appeared and disappeared with a clap of thunder. These occurrences happened many years ago, so a little investigation may be necessary before you are able to pin down the particulars.

Port Medway

One of the creepiest stories I've ever heard comes from here. It is said that late one evening, just before dark, a boat landed on the shore here, manned by a crew of headless sailors. They walked across the beach and disappeared into the dark woods. For many years, locals would not go near this spot at night and travellers were warned off spending any time there.

Lunenburg County

Dublin Bay

A ghost ship, locally named the Fire Ship, appears every seven years. The rattling of chains and singing of the sailors can clearly be heard. It is said that the ship appears so the ghostly crew can bury their ill-gotten treasure along the shore. No one knows for sure why the ship and its crew appears every seven years, but ghostly appearances every seventh year are a common feature of folktales from around the world, and South Shore folklore in particular. In the most famous ghost story of all, and my personal favourite, *A Christmas Carol* by Charles Dickens, Jacob Marley appears seven years after his death to his former partner, Ebenzer Scrooge, to warn him to change his nefarious, ungenerous ways.

Indian Island

Offshore from Broad Cove, this small island boasts a frightening manifestation of the connection between ghosts and buried treasure. The earth shakes and deep rumblings come out of the ground at certain times of the year. Even worse, a regiment of soldiers emerges from the ground in defence of treasure that was buried on the island many years ago. A French outpost stood on the mainland, and concerned about possible attack, they buried their gold and valuables on this small island. They must have fled the area quickly without retrieving their treasure, for the restless spirits of those stationed there are still on guard.

Green Bay

Another fire ship, this time a smaller sloop, is believed to make its appearance every seven years near here, also connected with rumours of buried treasure. The crew can be heard talking amongst themselves as the ship drops anchor, then the ship disappears.

In August 1885, a sea serpent made Green Bay his home for two days. Described as "a hideous length of undulating terror," the serpent was between forty and fifty feet in length, had a long mane of hair, a huge head and saucer-shaped eyes.

LaHave River

Local legend has it that the unquiet spirit of Captain Kidd sails ups the river every seven years in a vessel ablaze with lights. So many lights, in fact, the type of vessel is indiscernible to any observer. It appears only once, and only during the summer months when the night is warm with little wind blowing. It is believed that Kidd returns to find his treasure since folklore states that every seven years a buried treasure must come up to the surface for a short time before sinking back down into its hiding place.

Conquerall Bank

At Conquerall Bank on the LaHave River come reports of mysterious lights as well. However, these ones are not connected with ghost ships or pirate treasure. Instead, they are believed to be the spirits of criminals eternally condemned to haunt the place of their lawless lifestyle. They restlessly bob back and forth along the shore on dark, moonless nights, perhaps awaiting a shipment of stolen goods that will never come.

Other lights are seen going up the hill at Conquerall Bank, and these ones are believed to be the spirits of two neighbours who fought over the boundary line between their property. The lights slowly ascend the hill separately, then meet at the top and disappear in a blinding flash.

Rose Bay

There is a pond here haunted by a phantom ice skater. No one knows who he is, but skaters have been both impressed and terrified by his skill and daring on the ice.

Rose Bay/Kingsburg

A curious little story comes from the road between these two hamlets. The phantom of a goose appears and bites people on the legs. Years ago, many people would find their path blocked by this maniacal avian spectre and would return to their homes rather than tempt its wrath.

Lunenburg

Gallows Hill, as its name implies, once was home to a gallows, which saw ultimate punishment meted out. Today it is a graveyard and the home of Lunenburg Academy.

Gallows Hill is also reputed to be the burial ground for a werewolf that terrified residents in December 1755. A mysterious presence was felt in the woods and around the settlement at night. Animals were found torn apart and mysterious shadows lurked outside in the bushes of many homes. A child went missing and her father was found covered with blood, snarling like a mad dog, and had to be subdued by a group of men. The man apparently had murdered his own child and was secured in the local jail. The next morning he was found dead, having ripped out the veins in his arms. Needless to say, this shocking and gruesome series of events gave rise to talk of werewolves. The burial place of the werewolf of Lunenburg County is not marked, but perhaps the location has been passed down through the generations of the families of the men who buried the man-creature on the hill.

Lunenburg Academy is easily the most picturesque building in Lunenburg. However, it always had a slightly uneasy feeling associated with it as you pass below the hill and look up at it through the trees, especially in winter when the leaves are down and the bare branches frame the building like some gothic masterpiece. Being almost surrounded by a graveyard doesn't help keep the unease at bay. In keeping with the name of Gallows Hill and its location, Lunenburg Academy is, not surprisingly, reputed to be haunted. It has been difficult to pin down any specifics, but the feelings of something "not right" originate in the basement of this old building. It could just be the architecture of old buildings, but the oppressive atmosphere of the basement means that most students and staff do not venture down there alone.

The Fink-Holden House at 49 Cornwallis Street doesn't look any different from many other beautiful houses in this picturesque town. But it has one extra that not many of the other houses do. It is believed by some that the last surviving Holden family member won't let go of his former residence. And his determination began the very night he died. During that cold night in February 1996, the closet door of the master bedroom blew open suddenly, waking everyone in the house. Since that time the owner has felt a presence in the house, a presence he did not feel before the night Holden died.

A sea monster of tremendous size was sighted off Lunenburg in July of 1890. Terrified onlookers and fishermen claimed it was sixty yards long – fear may have caused them to say yards instead of feet – as they watched the beast swim leisurely around the harbour.

Blue Rocks

Blue Rocks is a picturesque community outside of Lunenburg and has the dubious honour of being one of the places in Nova Scotia with a legend of a headless rider. Children from Blue Rocks went to school in Lunenburg and this meant a long walk through the woods to town. Today that route is the Old Blue Rocks Road, but many years ago it wasn't paved and was a more arduous trip. Being an isolated road, it had its fair share of rumours about being haunted.

Surprisingly, this story occurred on a bright sunny day, rather than during the dark stormy nights that most ghosts prefer to haunt lonely roads. Arriving at school one morning, a scared young boy told his teachers he was walking to school when he heard the sounds of a horse coming up the road from behind him. Stepping off the road and turning to see who it was, the boy was terrified to see a huge black horse ridden by a man dressed all in black, and without a head. The boy took off into the woods, then ran the rest of the way to his school where he related this story to his teachers and fellow students.

Also along the road from Blue Rocks to Lunenburg is the ghostly sight of a team of oxen pulling a wagon. In it is a young couple out on a date that will last for eternity.

Sacrifice Island

Another horrifyingly titled location is that of Sacrifice Island. The name's origins are almost certainly folkloric rather than reality-based, but nevertheless, the island has enough mysterious phenomena to warrant a visit on a foggy night.

Local residents of nearby Heckman's Island report that strange lights appear on the uninhabited island just off their shores. Local legend has it that the lights are those of children who were sacrificed many years before. As well, indistinct phantoms are said to roam the island. Observers have also seen a headless spectre of a man in black about seven or eight feet tall. The witnesses to this strange sight were catching wild sheep on the island when they observed the apparition walking some distance away from them across a field, leaving twenty-one-inch tracks in the soft ground of the meadow.

Covey's Island

Covey's Island has had a sad, brutal history of death. Once called Payzant Island, four early settlers were murdered here. All that is left from these tragedies is a book by Linda Layton on the Payzant family (*A Passion for Survival: The True Story of Marie Anne and Louis Payzant in Eighteenth-Century Nova Scotia*), the crumbling remains of a foundation of the old house and a bloody handprint. In the throes of death one of the settlers, Louis Payzant, left his handprint in blood on a rock near the ruins of the house's foundation, where it remains to this day.

Martin's Brook

The chalets at Prince's Inlet Retreat are one of my refuges from this crazy world, especially when I want to write in peace. I highly recommend this place for the creatively blessed. Marilyn and Steven Hebb run a wonderful business here for the weary writer, though they never told me about this ghost story.

Long before the roads around here were paved and street-lights installed, gravel roads were the norm and the light of the moon was the only illumination for travellers from near-by Mahone Bay or Lunenburg. Along one of these roads many years ago two men were returning home late at night when they thought they heard the sinister sounds of low growling coming out of the blackness. This disturbing development continued as they walked towards Martin's Brook, constantly looking over their shoulders to see what was following them. Finally, almost mindless with fear, they ran the rest of the way home.

Months later, they heard of a similar experience that another late-night traveller had. A man on horseback was returning home the same way as the young men. Again there was a full moon, and again there were sounds of sinister growling coming from behind him. This time, however, whatever it was that had followed the two young men and now followed the rider on that lonely road attacked, throwing the rider from his horse. The attack was sudden and swift, lasting only a few seconds. Although he couldn't see what had set upon him, he believed it was a wild animal, so he quickly remounted his horse and rushed home. Reaching the safety of his house, he was amazed to see his clothing had been ripped by sharp claws, though he himself was untouched. The most disturbing aspect of the whole event was his inability to see his attacker, only to hear its menacing growls in the darkness.

Martin's River

The death of a local person is presaged in this area by a mysterious light, called the Jack o'Lantern, which appears at night and swings back and forth as if it was a lantern being carried by a man or woman as they walk along the road at night. People have tried to follow the light, but they could never catch up to it. The next day a report of someone dying would surely follow its appearance.

Mahone Bay

One June night in 1813, British warships chased an American privateer, *Young Teazer*, into Mahone Bay. The captain torched the magazine and the ship blew up. Since that time, some have seen a blazing ship sailing the bay at night during June and December. The December apparition could be related to the predecessor of *Young Teazer*, the *Teazer*, which was burned by British ships six months before the *Young Teazer* met her fate. There are also stories of a ball of fire crossing the bay, so it is possible both ships are making an appearance in the still of the night.

New Ross

The Grey Lady from the Annapolis Valley makes her appearance here in the deep, dark woods outside of New Ross. She is dressed in a long grey cloak and silently walks along the road, disappearing into the woods whenever a car approaches.

Oak Island

The causeway leading to Oak Island

Perhaps Nova Scotia's most renowned mystery is that of Oak Island. More precisely, it is the treasure rumoured to be buried on Oak Island that has captured the world's imagination. For two hundred years many people have searched and dug, and spent much money on this quest. This is their story.

In 1795, Daniel McInnis visited the island one day as a lark. Oak Island was mostly trees then, although some logging had been performed on the island. After walking through the forest, the teenager came upon a clearing. The clearing wasn't new, however, since saplings were growing in place of the trees that had been cut down. In the middle of the clearing was an old oak tree that had a branch which extended over a small depression in the ground. Accounts differ, but some say that there was an old tackle block hanging from the tree which crumbled to the ground when touched.

Daniel realized there was something buried there. Since Nova Scotia's coastline was often the haunt of many a sailor, he made the connection with treasure that has never been broken. The next day he returned with two friends by the name of Vaughan and Smith and they preceded to dig out the hole. On that day, the Money Pit, as it became known, began to capture their imagination and weave a complicated web.

The boys dug down ten feet before they reached a floor of decaying logs. Excited at this discovery, they pulled up the logs to discover more dirt below. Again they dug and at the twenty-foot level they again reached a platform of logs. Again they pulled these up and again there was dirt underneath. They finally dug down to the thirty-foot level and after pulling that platform of logs up they decided they needed more help. However, it wasn't until 1805 that they were able to convince people to resume the treasure hunt. And when they did all they found were more platforms of logs and a stone tablet that had mysterious markings on it. Some have tried to decipher the markings and one translation read, "Ten feet below, £2 million are buried."

Over the years many investors and groups started out with high hopes and good strategies, only to find their hopes dashed by a dose of reality. The table on page 78 lists the various groups, dates and major discoveries over the last two hundred years.

It became apparent early in the search that the works on Oak Island were of a highly complex nature, obviously designed by a capable engineer. For instance, there are several water tunnels designed to serve as a trap for anyone who dug deep enough to trigger them. Remaining dry until they were reached by searchers, the tunnels instantly began to let in water from the Atlantic Ocean, which floods almost every shaft sunk to get at the treasure. This work would have required over two years' effort by at least a hundred men, well beyond the capabilities, discipline and patience of anyone not connected with the military.

Over the years, while many theories and theorists have come and gone, the only constant has been the unshakable belief in the existence of a treasure. Regardless of what was actually

DATE	GROUP	DISCOVERIES
1803-1804	Onslow Co.	12-foot by 12-foot chamber at 100 feet
1849-1851	Truro Co.	possible chests, pieces of gold chain; built coffer dam to attempt to block sea tunnel
1861-1864	Oak Island Association	proved treasure chamber had dropped into large cavern
1866-1867	Oak Island Eldorado Co	tried to use coffer dam to block sea tunnel
1878	Sophie Sellers	
1893-1900	Oak Island Treasure Co.	cave-in pit, second water tunnel, reached depth of 170 feet
1909	Old Gold Salvage & Wrecking Co.	drilled to 167 feet
1931	Chappell	miner's seal-oil lamp, axe head, pick and anchor fluke
1936-1938	Hedden	stone triangle, collapsed water tunnel
1938-1944	Edwin H. Hamilton	explored water tunnels
1955	George J. Greene	pumped 100,000 gallons of water into pit which vanished
1959-1965	Robert Restall	found drains at the beach; Restall, his son and two others died of fumes in the pit
1965-1966	Robert Dunfield	practically dug out the island
1966-present	Triton Alliance	a chest and a floating hand were observed via TV around 170 feet.

buried on the island, it was of extreme importance to someone for them to go through the elaborate precautions of protecting it like this. It is unlikely that it is pirates' treasure, as pirates rarely held onto their money or booty long enough to bury it, let alone bury it so elaborately. Here are a few of the many theories that have emerged over the years.

Theory One

Certainly the oldest and most persistent theory of who buried what on Oak Island is that of Captain Kidd. Captain William Kidd was an English privateer who plied the waters of the Atlantic and Caribbean in the 1680s and '90s. In the late 1690s, he strayed over the line into the very act he was out to crush. This, as well as some political maneuvering and backstabbing, resulted in his arrest and sentence of death at the gallows. Just before he met his fate on May 23, 1701, Kidd wrote to the government informing them that he had hidden a great deal of treasure, and if they would let him live a little longer, he would lead them to it. This effort was in vain, and the sentence of death was carried out. This last plea from the condemned man has resulted in many a treasure hunt around the world and given Oak Island a ready culprit for the workings on the island.

Alas, it is unlikely Captain Kidd put anything on Oak Island. Firstly, the crews that Captain Kidd had were a mutinous, criminal bunch with little discipline, certainly not the discipline necessary to build the Money Pit. Secondly, Captain Kidd's time is almost totally accounted for by historians. There is no gap in the record for the amount of time it took to do what was done on Oak Island, estimated at two years. There is no evidence that Captain Kidd was anywhere near Oak Island at any time.

Theory Two

This theory is related to the first one. Some believe that other pirates buried a remarkable treasure on Oak Island. This theory is given some credence by those who know that pirates frequented Nova Scotia, particularly the LaHave River further down the coast. However, the classic scene of pirates burying their treasure is not entirely correct. Pirates spent more treasure than they ever buried, and after the few times they did bury some of their loot, they often came back for it.

That said, there have been small caches of unidentified treasure found from time to time, but nothing as large as the efforts on Oak Island would seem to indicate. Someone spent a lot of time and effort to hide something very large and/or valuable, not just any pickings from some ship. Added to this is the fact that not many pirates had the technical training, time or manpower to do something like Oak Island. Even the idea of a communal bank for pirates doesn't seem logical. Hidden money does no one any good. The whole reason for existence for a pirate was to spend money, not hide it. It is also doubtful that many pirates would trust one another enough to develop a communal bank for their treasure. As a final nail in the pirate communal bank coffin, no whispers or hints of such a thing have ever surfaced, and not all pirates died early deaths.

Theory Three

This theory is really a hard sell. You first have to believe that William Shakespeare didn't really write all those plays attributed to him. The theory is that Sir Francis Bacon did and that he felt he must hide his authorship of the plays for political reasons. Because of his Masonic connections with the major explorers and developers of the New World, he decided to hide the manuscripts on a deserted island far away from palace intrigue.

There is no evidence that Francis Bacon wrote any of Shakespeare's plays and sonnets, though some scholars seem to find it impossible to believe that someone with limited education and no great political connections could write the beautiful works that we believe William Shakespeare produced.

Now, even if I could subscribe to the theory that Francis Bacon really did the writing, I must believe he buried his manuscripts underground guarded by water tunnels. Paper … water, hmm. Doesn't seem logical to me, although some people throw the idea out that the manuscripts were secured in liquid mercury to preserve them. Still, the only evidence for the fact that there is something of a paper product down there is the tiny fragment of parchment brought up with one of the drills. I can think of a simpler reason why there would be a parchment. Perhaps there would be a manifest listing whatever is below and its worth. This is a far less complicated reason for finding paper down there.

As for the Masonic connections, practically everyone in power in England at that time, and the men they sent out to discover and develop the new lands, was a Mason. I don't think you could find an explorer during that period who wasn't a Mason or connected with one.

Theory Four

This theory is almost as complicated as the Bacon one, but at least it has circumstantial evidence backing it up. Essentially, it states that the treasure is from the Knights Templars, a religious sect that fought in the Crusades and became so rich that many of the monarchs of Europe went to them in time of financial need. In the fourteenth century, the King of France went to the Pope and convinced him to outlaw the Templars. In a sneak attack, the King's men stormed their castles and arrested, tortured and killed many of them. At the Templars' stronghold, they were able to hold out long enough to spirit some of their massive treasure away, and it has never been found.

Many Templars headed for Scotland and were welcome there. In 1395, Prince Henry Sinclair, the Earl of Orkney, likely made a transatlantic journey to Nova Scotia, and some scholars have tried for a connection between the Earl and the Templar treasure. However, nothing is certain, although much of it is plausible and could have happened that way.

In the 1980s, a new theory emerged that said the Holy Grail was actually the sacred bloodline of Jesus of Nazareth, not a cup or chalice. A variation on the theme of the Templars has them hiding either the Holy Grail, the chalice of the last supper, or the Holy Grail, the bloodline (descendants) of Jesus Christ. There is also a theory that the container holding the Shroud of Turin is the fabled Holy Grail. Again, there is circumstantial evidence to link the Templars to the descendants of Jesus Christ and secret societies, and Samuel de Champlain. Coincidentally, Champlain was meticulous in his charting of the region of the Maritimes, yet he became vague about the area around Oak Island.

Theory Five

This theory contends that a pay ship of the British, French or Spanish navy was caught in a storm and washed ashore near Oak Island. The commanders decided to bury the treasure until they could return with a stronger force. Although pay ships of the various navies did founder along the Atlantic coast of North America, and one French ship did make for Bedford Basin, there is no evidence to directly link any missing money and the diggings on Oak Island.

Theory Six

A variation on theory five is that the French felt their holdings in Acadia were in jeopardy and hid some of their money until things cleared up. Of course when they did, the French were out.

Another variation is that the English did much the same, or hid some of the money they would need to fight the American colonists. If this theory were true, why didn't they ever come back for it? Nova Scotia was always under their control and they could have come and retrieved the treasure at any time.

Theory Seven

This theory again is very similar to the "hide the stuff until it's safe" theories, except that those burying the treasure wanted it safe from the tax man.

This argument holds that after the Sack of Havana in 1752, the leaders of the successful British invasion-cum-looting of Havana, Cuba, decided to skim off some of the take before sending it back to King George the Third. A variation along these lines is that the king didn't trust his ministers and wanted some money hidden away for a royal emergency. Eventually, however, the money was forgotten. But what of the men who organized and buried the treasure?

Who? What?

I have not included every theory as to who buried what on Oak Island. I purposely left out the fantastic, impossible or ridiculous, and concentrated on the theories that at least had a chance of being right, even if the Bacon one is a real stretch.

The person who dreamed up this adventure, planned and engineered it and executed the world's greatest secular mystery was military or pseudo-military. By this, I would probably reject the Templars as well as Bacon. This was a military job by either the French or, more likely, the British. It took two years and massive manpower to construct a trap for the curious. Obviously, it was designed so the treasure could not be retrieved the same way it was hidden. There is some trick to it and it is possible, even likely, that the treasure ended up a short distance away just under the ground ready for easy access.

The Money Pit is meant as a trap to take the curious off the scent. Even the likely treasure chests found through the drilling were probably a sacrificial lamb in case anyone succeeded in getting down that far. Can you imagine going through all this trouble for two treasure chests? No, whatever was or is on Oak Island must have been massive, either in wealth or importance.

The only way to find out who put the treasure there on the island is to search history for the likely suspects: the men who had the capability and disappeared for about two years. Find them and you find the likely reason for their efforts. Understand the reason for their efforts, and you have the treasure, at least in your mind. It is possible that the treasure could only be found by unravelling the clues scattered throughout the island, and perhaps at some time in the past, someone did.

Does it not strike anyone how something of this magnitude could stay a secret for so long? Someone must have told someone. Husbands tell wives or families. Families leave letters or papers behind after deaths. There has never been a mention or whisper of the treasure. We have no idea what it is. Therefore, either the men who buried it did not know what it was they were burying, or else they came back and got it.

The questions surrounding buried treasure have long overshadowed other mysterious phenomena on the island. It is said that a large, black, red-eyed dog patrols the island looking for interlopers. The dog has been described as being as big as a small horse and his eyes burn like red-hot coals. Some believe the dog to be the spirit of a long-dead pirate who was sacrificed to protect the treasure, while others insist it is the Devil himself.

Also seen on Oak Island are the ghostly apparitions of sixteenth- and seventeenth-century soldiers. They walk the roads, woods and beaches, still guarding or searching for something.

Pirate apparitions are seen or heard from time to time on the lonely island too. Are they the ones who buried something here, still looking for their treasure?

Chester

There are many fine inns along the South Shore, and some of the most interesting are those around Chester. One in particular boasts more than its share of charm, if you find a ghost a charming addition, that is.

Haddon Hall sits atop a hill overlooking the town, but it is not as scary looking as the haunted houses Hollywood portrays in similar situations. There are no winding roads with dead trees leading up to the inn, but there is a resident ghost to keep you company. Staff at the inn believes the ghost to be a former owner of the building who stops by on occasion to keep an eye on her earthly residence. She is also said to keep watch over the cleaning staff to see that they do a good job. She has even been credited with warning the owner that her pet cockatoo was in danger of freezing to death. As some ghosts go, this one is pretty benign.

The Mill Cove Brook meanders through the northern section of "downtown" Chester and the stone bridge that spans it figures prominently in local legend. Two hundred years ago, Nova Scotia was a rough place with death never that far away. In the various towns that dotted the South Shore were taverns where drinking and gambling got out of hand with unfortunate results for some. During a heated argument over cards one cold winter's night, a traveller lost more than the argument and his body was thrown into the icy waters of Mill Cove Brook by the wooden bridge which then spanned it. The decomposing body of the unfortunate traveller wasn't discovered until warmer weather set in and children began to swim and fish by the bridge.

The killers were never prosecuted. Many believe that because of this, the spirit of the poor man will never rest. Reports soon came in about a mysterious white "something" that was seen climbing out of the water and up the wooden bridge. Needless to say, people crossing the bridge did so quicker than normal and with bated breath. This "something" continued its climb even after the wooden bridge was replaced by a stone structure in the late 1800s. Though recent reports are scarce, I'd still love to cross it on a foggy night, pausing to listen for any sound of the restless dead.

On the Number 3 Highway between Chester and East Chester appears the phantom of an elderly nun. No one knows who she was or why she still walks the old road, but some speculate her last wishes were not carried out and she cannot rest until they are.

Marriott's Cove

Here, a house has ghostly footsteps that climb the stairs every night, accompanied by a cold spot, that traditional indicator of a spectral presence.

Little Tancook Island

A mysterious bright light appears near this island before a major storm. It could also be related to legends of buried treasure on the island. The light is said to be stationary, yet not connected with anything solid or identifiable.

Halifax Regional Municipality

St. Margaret's Bay

In 1845, sightings of a very large "sea serpent" were reported to the local press. Two men in a schooner noticed what appeared to be a tangle of nets in the water on the west side of the Bay. Suddenly the "net" straightened itself out and began to move away from the boat under its own power. It was estimated the creature was about seventy to one hundred feet long, steel grey in colour, and with a head the size of a barrel. It also had a long mane.

This was not the only sighting of the creature, for in 1849 a similar beast appeared, though this one was estimated to be only sixty feet in length. It also differed from the earlier creature in that it had a row of spines, about one inch long, down the length of its body, which was tapered like an eel's and black in colour. This creature was more aggressive than the last, for when it saw that it was being observed by two men in a rowboat, it raised its head, displayed a red mouth with long teeth, and followed the boat almost to shore.

Big Indian Lake

North of French Village Station is a series of dams and lakes. Many years ago five people, two women and three men, drowned near Big Indian Lake dam and at least one of those unfortunate souls is not at rest. Boaters have seen a man in a rubber coat and sou'wester walking endlessly along the top of the dam.

Glen Haven

The restless soul of a murdered man appears in the form of a big black dog with huge red eyes running through the woods here.

Seabright

One of the rare occasions when two ghostly women appear at the same time occurs here at Seabright. These spectres show themselves at night, dressed wholly in black with black hats, and glisten in the moonlight. They are tall, silent and walk along the road together.

Glen Margaret

A man was once hanged from a poplar tree here. It is said that the spirits of those who are hanged cannot leave their bodies. Whatever the truth, since the time of the hanging a small yellow dog has appeared, ignores everyone and everything, and just walks along the road to the place where the tree once stood, then disappears. Local superstition has it the dog is the Devil, who was cheated out of the man's spirit when he was hung.

Hackett's Cove

Another headless ghost appears here at Devany's Brook. The spectre of a headless woman comes out of the water occasionally with something white over her like a sheet.

As well, in the eastern part of St. Margaret's Bay, the ghostly vision of a Spanish ship appears once a year. It is first seen coming from the direction of Peggy's Cove. It sails to Red Bank, over to Northwest Cove, and then exits the Bay. It makes its appearance in the early fall, sometimes on fire.

Shut-In Island

Shut-In Island was originally known as Chetigne Island, and before that, Pirate's Island. It is the latter name that concerns us here. As we have seen, the South Shore of Nova Scotia was a haven for pirates. Although they usually confined themselves to the area around the LaHave River, stories have come down to us about other areas they may have visited. One of these other areas is present-day Shut-In Island. Over the years many vessels were wrecked on the island or the reef that joins it to the mainland.

Legend has it that some of these ships were pirate ships and their crews were forced to bury their ill-gotten loot on the island until they could arrange to come back and get it.

Another story coming out of Shut-In Island is a mysterious light seen at certain times only from the mainland. The reporting of strange lights on the island would seem to be only natural considering its reputation. There has long been a belief that pirates would murder someone and bury him with their treasure so that the ghost of the murdered man would scare anyone away from the hoard. So it is not surprising that some would see a light coming from the island.

Indian Harbour

Passing through this very peaceful and picturesque village outside of Peggy's Cove, one wouldn't think it was filled with some of the most spine-tingling stories of the province. The first concerns the ghost of a fisherman who is seen along Middle Point Road. Locals assume he is heading to the harbour, and he is seen pushing a wheelbarrow, though no one can ever get close enough to see what the contents are.

The next story concerns a fiery spirit who appears in the waters of Indian Harbour. A spectral Mi'kmaq maiden can be seen standing in the water by the shore, consumed with flames, and with her arms and head raised towards heaven as if to be spared this eternal horror.

Finally, along the desolate and rocky shore walks the lonely spirit of a Scottish lady in a blue dress. She came to Nova Scotia to marry and have children by a fisherman, but he died while out at sea, leaving her and her children alone. For some reason, his family would have nothing to do with them, a state of affairs that haunted her and increased her grief and unhappiness. Now, from beyond the grave, her spirit still walks along the shore, as sad and lonely in death as she was in life.

Sambro

At Sambro Light a Scottish soldier once hanged himself, and his ghost can still be seen as wispy trails of blackish mist. The full story of Double Alex appears in the Maritime Museum of the Atlantic entry on page 99 since that is the place where he is most often seen. As well as witnessing the rare visitation of this doomed soldier, visitors to the Light might hear casks being thrown around in the bottom of the lighthouse and the pitiful cries of shipwrecked people blowing in from the sea.

More than 250 years ago a strange creature was pulled out of the water here. Called a giant sea turtle at the time, it sounds quite different than any turtle of any size. Said to be as big as an ox with short brownish hair and loose, rough skin, it had a bull-like neck and its head resembled an alligator's, with teeth ten inches long. Apparently, it died of injuries received in a battle with another aquatic creature, for its stomach was ripped open as if bitten by some large animal.

Also at Sambro is a small island where pirates buried their dead. It is said that the place where they were buried has no grass growing on it. Other islands have been searched for treasure around here, but this little island is untouched for fear that the dead pirates will rise up against anyone who might disturb them.

Chebucto Head

The Chebucto Head lighthouse is one of my favourite places to go to relax and get out of the city for a while. On the water side you have wave-swept rocks like Peggy's Cove, and on the other a moor straight out of Arthur Conan Doyle's *The Hound of the Baskervilles.*

The lighthouse is now unmanned like many of Nova Scotia's venerable lighthouses, so it is difficult to determine whether the ghostly lady still walks the cliffs nearby. Although not much is known about the ghost, it is believed she was a shipwreck victim

Chebucto Head

due to the thick rope tied around her waist. Some of the former lightkeepers saw her regularly out on the wave-lashed rocks, lost and alone for eternity.

The approaches to Halifax Harbour are home to two different types of mysterious sights. The first is that of our common ghost ship, though with all the ships that have come and gone into the harbour over the centuries you would think we would have a ghost freighter, submarine or destroyer to add some local flavour. On foggy nights a fully rigged sailing vessel is seen gliding silently into the harbour. It is also been seen passing McNab's Island and even as far in as Navy Island on the eastern side of Bedford Basin. This ship is believed to be one from Duc d'Anville's fleet.

Many years ago when wooden ships were gradually being replaced with iron-built ones, a mysterious iron ship was found drifting aimlessly without any crew just outside the harbour. It appeared as if everyone just put down what they were doing and disappeared. Her home port was Liverpool, England, so arrangements were made to sail her back home. On the voyage back the new crew discovered a box with a watch and a lady's clothes inside. Some believe she was murdered, but even if that had happened, it doesn't explain what happened to the crew. Why would everyone abandon ship within sight of Halifax? What became of them?

Clay Hill

Just down the road from the Chebucto Head/Duncan's Cove area is Clay Hill. This area has some frightening stories associated with it, yet most people don't even know the name. Strange lights have been seen on top of the hill or weaving through the woods. Sounds of an invisible boat being rowed ashore or of chains rattling are common when the night is dark and close. Figures of people can be seen walking through the woods or along the road, but they leave no footprints or marks in the snow.

Terence Bay

The Bog Lady is one of my favourite stories. There is a legend around here that a lonely lady hermit once lived in the woods off the road near a bog. Though harmless, she was feared by the local children and had a disturbing habit of walking along the side of the road at night, so often drivers would come across this dirty vision as they rounded a sharp corner on their way home. One night a red car speeding down the road came around the corner and hit and killed the poor woman. Some local residents claim she was hurriedly buried in the woods and rests uneasily. Rumour has it that if you drive down the Terence Bay Road at a full moon in a red car doing a hundred kilometres an hour, she will appear in your backseat.

Another ghost frequently seen in this quiet community is an apparition of an old man that walks down the centre line of the Terence Bay Road. He appears suddenly at night, giving a driver just enough time to swerve around him. At times, however, this has been impossible and when the shaken and distraught motorist walks back to search for a body, none can be found.

Halifax

Bridge Curse

A Mi'kmaq medicine man put a curse on three bridges to be built joining the twin cities of Halifax and Dartmouth. The first was to fall in a storm, the second calmly and the third in death.

On September 7, 1891, a hurricane hit Halifax Harbour with winds up to 112 kilometres per hour. Much damage was done to the harbour docks and a large portion of the bridge built in 1884 collapsed during the night. Over a quarter of a mile long and up to fifty feet wide, it was mainly a railway bridge with a footpath along the track and a steel swing section near the Dart-

Angus L. Macdonald Bridge

mouth shore which opened to let ships move in and out of Bedford Basin.

After lengthy deliberations, a second bridge was built in the same location, but this time using piles pounded into The Narrows seabed for support. This bridge appeared unstable after completion, so granite blocks were placed on the seabed beside the bridge and connected with cables to make it more secure. Despite these efforts, the second bridge floated away on July 6, 1893, after a strong tide essentially lifted it from its foundation on a quiet summer night.

When it came time to open the third bridge, the Angus L. Macdonald Bridge, authorities asked the Mi'kmaq chief of the time to remove the curse. It apparently worked. The bridge has stood solidly since it was built in the 1950s. Jay Underwood points out in *Ghost Tracks: Surprising Stories of the Supernatural on Rails* that the first two bridges crossed The Narrows and thus the Angus L. Macdonald Bridge wouldn't be the one to fall, but instead, it would be the "new bridge" built in 1970, the A. Murray MacKay Bridge, which actually crosses The Narrows. Underwood also found out the curse is a recent invention. Still, it takes a brave heart for many to cross the "old bridge" without a flicker of unease.

Halifax Harbour

At various times in the city's history strange aquatic creatures have been spotted all along the harbour and Bedford Basin. A sixty-foot serpentine creature was sighted at the foot of the George Street pier in 1825. Looking like a huge log and keeping its head about three feet out of the water, it startled nearby citizens. A few dozen witnesses watched as it passed the pier and one witness counted eight humps. This may be the same monster seen at the harbour approaches occasionally.

Also seen prowling the harbour on dark, foggy nights is a French ship-of-the-line, apparently one of the survivors of the disastrous Duc d'Anville's task force.

George's Island

George's Island is the small island in the middle of the harbour, near Pier 21. A part of the ring of fortifications that surrounded the old city, George's Island was off limits to the general public for many years. As such, its charms and mysteries have remained untouched over the years. Most people don't even know it has a rich assortment of ghostly activity.

Perhaps the most famous spectre of George's Island is Duc d'Anville. Jean-Baptiste-Louis Frédéric de La Rochefoucauld de Roye, Duc d'Anville was the French admiral in command of an expedition that set out from France in 1746 to retake Louisbourg, which had been captured by the British. Storms, disease and bad luck meant the tattered fleet had to put into Chebucto Bay – Halifax Harbour. D'Anville himself died just after they arrived, either by poison or suicide. His grand fleet lay in ruins with many ships sunk or unable to take part in any battle. He was buried temporarily on what was to be named George's Island.

The fleet returned to France. After the establishment of Halifax in 1749, the French were allowed to collect the remains of the admiral and rebury him at Louisbourg. But the spirit of the admiral is said to walk the shoreline of George's Island, his first resting place and the place of his greatest despair. One labourer in the nineteenth century claimed to have witnessed a ghostly re-enactment of his burial on a quiet September morning.

D'Anville's spectre is also said to cross the harbour to the Halifax shoreline and walk all the way to Rockingham on the shores of Bedford Basin, the site of many graves of his beloved sailors from that doomed expedition. The ghost is accompanied by the sounds of groaning wooden ships and spectral sails flapping in the wind. The place where he disappears was once called French Landing and when the British came three years later, they were greeted by the awful sight of rotted corpses in the uniforms of French sailors and soldiers. Since that time many have suggested that somewhere close by is buried treasure from the fleet's pay ship, awaiting the day when another fleet would put into Chebucto Bay in preparation to retake Louisbourg.

Another long-time superstition regarding George's Island states that in the quiet, still moments before dawn, the dead arise from the small island and cross over the harbour to walk the streets and linger in taverns long destroyed.

What would an area of Nova Scotia be without a wandering ghostly woman? The island is the final resting place of many people, military and civilian, and so it is uncertain who this woman was. A woman unlucky in love? A victim of disease banished to the island? Whoever she was, she is seen wandering the shoreline looking towards Dartmouth, dressed in wet grey clothes with seaweed clinging to her. The Lady in Grey is one of the oldest ghost stories of Halifax, beginning just after its establishment and probably lasting well into the future.

Finally, it has been reported that the ghost of a one-armed French soldier can be seen sitting on the shore looking out of the harbour. Perhaps he was left behind when the fleet retreated to France and eternally awaits their return.

Historic Properties

Historic Properties is a collection of old buildings on the Halifax waterfront that have been restored to their original condition. They are a great tourist attraction with many shops, restaurants, bars and offices. They also have a few ghosts. In the building that houses the Lower Deck lounge, there is a ghostly shadow of a man seen upstairs in the offices when they are almost deserted and quiet. There have also been whisperings of other entities having been seen over the years, but they are proving harder to track down.

If there is a ghost at Historic Properties it almost certainly is that of Enos Collins (1774-1871), The well-known rough and ready Halifax businessman was one of the richest men in Canada. His Halifax Banking Company eventually became part of the Canadian Imperial Bank of Commerce.

You can get a good feeling of those earlier times as you walk through Historic Properties, and during a typical foggy Halifax night, when the mist is heavy upon the ground and sound reverberates between the ancient buildings, the ghosts may be easy to find.

Maritime Museum of the Atlantic

The museum has only been at its present location since 1982, but already it has its share of lingering spirits. Ghostly footsteps, cold spots, and unexplained occasions when lights turn on or go off of their own accord abound here. A few years ago when I was hosting the television series *Shadow Hunter*, we filmed an interview on ghost ships here. I was hoping that we might be lucky enough to see or hear one or the other of the museum's resident ghosts.

The first ghost said to be haunting the museum is that of James Farquhar, a sea captain whose statue once graced a window overlooking the foyer. Staff complained that the eyes of the statue followed them as they walked by, so it was moved to a less visible location. Little is known of James Farquhar and less of why he haunts the museum.

The second ghost is believed to be that of soldier Alex Alexander, often called Double Alex. He lived during the time of the American Revolution and was responsible for guarding the Sambro Lighthouse. He did not die in battle, but in shame. He was given the responsibility of travelling to Halifax to procure supplies, an important duty during that time when Sambro was a much longer trip than today with our modern roads. Alexander was a wastrel, and instead of obtaining the needed supplies, he spent the money drinking and gambling. After he sobered up, he returned to the lighthouse and hanged himself in shame. His ghost was said to haunt the lighthouse for years. When the lighthouse was automated, the light was brought to the museum. The spirit of Alex Alexander followed the light and now resides here. Perhaps it is his footsteps that are heard here late at night.

Art Gallery of Nova Scotia

The present site of the well-respected Art Gallery of Nova Scotia was once the location of the first gallows in Halifax. The first man to swing from the new gallows was a character named Peter Carteel, who deservedly died for the murder of Abraham Goodsides in the summer of 1749, the year Halifax was founded. Halifax's first public hanging and Carteel's final moments are re-played over and over again by the main doors of the gallery.

Halifax Club

The Halifax Club, located at 1682 Hollis Street and estab-lished in 1862, is one of Halifax's oldest and most prestigious clubs. No one knows for sure how many ghosts haunt the club, or their identities, but there are many suspects. One member killed himself, while another died while cheating on his wife. There is also a female presence seen there, so perhaps the spirit of the mistress of the cheating member feels repentant and can-not move on. After he expired, it is said, she put him in a cab and sent him to the club. Maybe they are together in death, walking the halls and rooms of the Halifax Club.

Illicit lovers are not the only spirits that haunt the premises. A mother and son call the club home, though members are un-sure as to why that is. When renovations were being made af-ter a major fire in 1995, workmen could hear the sounds of peo-ple walking up the stairs or running on the second floor, even though there was no one else in the building. Shadows moving on the stairs and the smell of fresh tobacco smoke are also com-mon. Most of the mysterious phenomena seem to occur between midnight and seven in the morning, so apparently the ghosts like to have the place to themselves.

Scotia Square/Granville Square

In the late 1960s, when many old buildings, houses and even streets disappeared from the heart of downtown Halifax, much of the city's history and heritage was lost. This area is the oldest developed part of Halifax and consisted of Jacob and Starr Streets, Hurd Lane, and Poplar Grove. The modern edifices that replaced them sit atop one of the areas of Halifax that has the longest lineage of mysterious phenomena.

At the corner of Hurd Lane and Water Street, near where a little park at the end of Granville Square sits today, there once was a red house that had problems keeping boarders, even during World War Two when lodging was at a premium. After a woman was murdered in this house, a spectre in white could be regularly seen prowling the halls and a strange presence of someone unseen could often be felt. The spectre would walk by the residents carrying a lamp and disappear at the rear of the house, endlessly searching for something that she could never find.

Another house in the vanished residential neighbourhood that is now the Cogswell Street Interchange next to Scotia Square had no problems with keeping owners, but the hired staff wouldn't stay for very long. Divided into flats, this square old house often gave servants a feeling of someone standing just behind them, even when they were alone in an empty room. From time to time, a woman in white would be seen reflected in some polished surface or hanging mirror.

Five Fishermen Restaurant

The Five Fishermen is one of the finer eating establishments in the province, and this author has spent many a birthday meal enjoying the excellent food and hospitality, quite unaware that he could have been watched over by the resident ghost.

The spirit said to reside in the restaurant is a ghost with an attitude. Most ghosts are content to quietly maintain their presence, but this one lets the staff know when it is around. It calls out staff members' names, trips them sometimes, and has even locked one employee in a room.

St. Paul's Anglican Church

During the Halifax Explosion of 1917 many buildings were damaged in the downtown. One of them was St Paul's, one of the oldest churches in North America. It still bears scars from the explosion, including a piece of metal from the *Mont Blanc*, the French munitions ship that collided with the Belgian Relief vessel *Imo*, causing the blast. There is another scar the church is more known for, however. One of the glass windows on Argyle Street was broken, and the silhouette of a man wearing a high hat can be seen. Local legend has it that the head of the parish minister went through the window during the explosion, but officials at the church would only say that the image bears an uncanny likeness to the minister at that time.

Citadel Hill

Today the impressive fortification that looks down upon Halifax and its harbour is but the latest in a long line of fortifications built on the site shortly after the city was founded in 1749. The Citadel of today is the fourth to stand on top of the hill and has been in a constant state of renovation since the mid-1980s. Few tourists travel to Halifax without going to the Citadel and taking in the views, or crossing through the gates and immersing themselves in the impressively recreated atmosphere of another time. There may be other remnants of a forgotten age here as well. A place with a history as long as this one has to have some mystery associated with it.

The Garrison Cells are the most famous of the Citadel's haunted places. It is said that the ghost of a long-ago prisoner can be heard and seen here. Staff members do not like being left alone in the section of the Citadel entitled The Tides of History, which is a display laid out to show the history of the fort, and some have heard their names being called when no one is around. Footsteps of people who can't be seen are coupled with the sounds of doors opening and closing by themselves.

There are also reports of strange shapes and shadows of invisible people all around the fort, but the most interesting experience occurred at Theatre Four where staff observed the shape of a person's head and shoulders in front of the security camera, even though the camera is ten feet off the floor. Staff used to be shy when talking about the mysterious phenomena at the old fort, but now they give Ghost Walks during the summer season and most employees are now quite happy to include a little supernatural flavour to the history of this grand place.

Finally, the ghost of a one-armed sergeant can be seen near Casement 18, on the north side of the Citadel. There is an un-used well behind the door of Casement 18 where the unfortunate sergeant drowned under suspicious circumstances during a fire at the fortification.

Brunswick Street

It's not often that a whole street is reputed to be haunted. Most ghostly activity is confined to a specific location. But if we are to believe the local folklore, Brunswick Street is haunted by the spectre of a young orphan boy who plays a flute mournfully in the night. In life he used to play his flute for his supper and was cruelly murdered one night. Since that time his plaintive notes can be heard drifting on the wind along this historic street.

Neptune Theatre

Many theatres boast their own ghost, and the old Neptune is no different, though not everyone agrees about his identity. Some think he was a vaudeville actor, but others believe he was an unfortunate sailor who fell to his death from above the stage. Regardless of who he really was, staff call him Syd From the Grid. His usual manifestation took the form of ghostly footsteps.

He was heard on the roof outside as well as the aisles inside. There's no word on whether Syd stayed with the troupe when they renovated the theatre.

Spring Garden Road Library

The Halifax Regional Memorial Library on Spring Garden Road is an old and atmospheric place. There is a statue of Sir Winston Churchill on the lawn out front, just past the street musicians, and the whole area is a beautiful place for Haligonians to hang out on warm, bright days. But inside it is a different story. Reports come to us that the library has its resident ghost. Although many libraries report a spirit of a former librarian, this ghost is not so identified. Staff and patrons report seeing shapes and shadows of people who couldn't possibly be there, which then disappear quickly. After closing, the sounds of someone moving about and deep breathing echo through the building. The library building has many twists and turns with plenty of shadowy corners for ghosts to hide in.

Spring Garden Road Courthouse

The attic of this grand old building at 5250 Spring Garden Road, built in the Classical Revival style and first opened in 1860, is a dark, musty and foreboding place. Staff have told me they refuse to go to it. The sounds of someone moving around when it is supposed to be empty have been reported and one janitor quit after swearing he saw eyes staring out at him from the disassembled pieces of the old gallows, last used in the 1930s.

Old Burial Ground

Once the literal end of the road – for the south end of the original city ended at the present-day junction of Barrington Street and Spring Garden Road – the Old Burial Ground (or Old Burying Ground) is reported to have over ten thousand bodies buried in it. The Old Burial Ground used to be much bigger, taking in the grounds of the Old Courthouse, Spring Garden Road Library and St. Mary's Basilica parking lot.

One of my favourite moments when I take local students on a "ghost tour" of the downtown comes when I point out that they walk over the dead whenever they are in this area. Those who walk these streets daily shouldn't worry, though. The dead rarely visit their burial site. In fact, very few actual hauntings occur in cemeteries, Hollywood and television notwithstanding. And in keeping with this fact, I haven't heard anything substantial reported in connection with the Old Burial Ground until recently, and I am not sure about its source. Nevertheless, I include it here for your information.

The Old Burial Ground has a rich and storied past, and many soldiers and heroes were buried here between 1749 and 1843. Some have seen the spectre of a military man walking amongst the tombstones, head held high and back straight as if on eternal parade.

1359 Barrington Street

This building is occupied by the Nova Scotia Association of Architects (NSAA). Previously, it housed the medical offices of a dermatologist, and before that it was a private residence. When it was a doctor's office, many of the staff refused to go upstairs because of the recurring ghostly cries of a baby. Also, many of the pictures refused to stay on the walls and would be found lying on the floor. This was more than enough for the staff to avoid going upstairs.

Waverley Inn

The Waverley Inn, located at 1266 Barrington Street, is diagonally across from the NSAA building and is one of the more charming inns in Halifax. A famous guest appears from time to time, more than a hundred years after he visited the city in the flesh.

Oscar Wilde was a household name when he visited Halifax in October 1882 to deliver two lectures, "The Decorative Arts" and "The House Beautiful," at the Academy of Music. The British dramatist was on a North American tour, and he lodged at the Waverley Inn during his three-night stay. A follower of the Aesthetic Movement, promoting the idea of "art for art's sake," Wilde was a flamboyant character in dress and mannerisms.

About 1,800 people in total attended his two lectures in Halifax, giving Wilde a good reception. He in turn praised the stage decorations. He promised to return one day, and although he did not keep that promise while alive, he has kept it after death. Staff and visitors have reported seeing an apparition that is garishly dressed, often reading a book, in the room Wilde occupied during his time in Halifax.

Henry House

This establishment at 1222 Barrington Street has long been a popular eating place and watering hole. Still keeping a Victorian charm, it is easy to imagine it might have a resident spirit or two. And it does.

The phantom of a servant girl has been seen on the stairway of the main entrance and another phantom woman can be seen standing in the driveway. Unexplained lights and sounds are seen and heard at odd times of day. Staff members have felt someone tapping them on the shoulder when no one is around. Names are called out when the place is empty of anyone but the observer, and in one terrifying experience, a disembodied face was seen hovering in the kitchen. Most of the phenomena are centred in the basement pub area.

Brewery Market

Today the Brewery Market on Lower Water Street is filled with small shops, atriums, restaurants and offices, and a Saturday farmers' market, but it began as the brewing house for Alexander Keith, a famous nineteenth-century brew-master of Nova Scotia. Even though he died in 1873, his ghost has been seen walking through the complex by some of the caretakers.

All Saints Cathedral

This beautiful cathedral has seen more than its share of visitors over the years, including one from beyond the grave. On New Year's Day, 1933, the dean of All Saints Cathedral, John Plummer Derwent Llwyd, was hit by a car as he made his way to comfort a parishioner who was at death's door. Dean Llwyd died a few months after the accident because of a blood clot resulting from his injuries. Since this time, parishioners have spoken of seeing Dean Llwyd going about his routines as if still blessed with life. He has been seen looking out at his congregation, walking along the altar, and striding up the aisle, still concerned with his earthly duties.

In at least one instance, a parishioner watched Dean Llwyd step off the altar and disappear. Another parishioner was surprised when Dean Llwyd walked by him while he was playing the organ. The ghost is selective with his manifestations, as he appears only during Sunday Service and has appeared coming out of the vestry door during the hymn "Down Ampney, Come down, O love divine."

Victoria General Hospital

Although staff members rarely discuss it, most hospitals report supernatural phenomena. Since the supernatural and electrical fields are closely correlated, especially in the cases of hallucinations, it is only natural that highly electrified places like hospitals report mysterious phenomena. Electromagnetic energy can cause hallucinations in susceptible people.

I used to work at the old Halifax Infirmary on Queen Street and loved hearing from the older employees about their experiences. From that job I developed a love of old buildings during the off peak hours when there is a residual presence from the busy day, but a quietness of approaching night.

A residual presence from a former time also exists at the Victoria General Hospital. There have been sightings of an elderly nun, clad wholly in grey, walking the halls or standing in patients' rooms.

Tower Road School

On December 6, 1917, the largest man-made explosion prior to the first nuclear explosion occurred in The Narrows section of Halifax Harbour. It destroyed most of the North End of the city, killed 2,000 people and left many more homeless. Many of the injured were taken to city schools and Tower Road School was used as a makeshift morgue. The apparition of a male teenager has been seen climbing the stairs to the attic, as well as walking through the basement. Footsteps are also heard in the deserted school and legend has it the ghost is that of a youth killed in the Halifax Explosion and brought there for processing. Maybe he was unidentified and is still waiting for his family to come and claim him.

University of King's College

Two spectres haunt this respected institution. In Alexandra Hall the wraith of a girl in white can be seen floating along an upper floor hallway. In an area under the Chapel known as the Pit, the ghost of a janitor wearing a yellow work jacket has been observed moving around.

Robie Street Palace

This white house, the second from the intersection of Jubilee Road and Robie Street, heading north along Robie, used to be a manor house on a piece of land encompassing the whole block. It was the residence of the first mayor of Halifax, William Caldwell, and was built in classic Doric style. For years it has had the reputation of being haunted, especially one side of the house, which had a blackened window.

One legend has it that someone hanged himself in the room just behind the blackened window, and ever since that time, the window will turn to black no matter how many times it is changed. Another story has it that witches, dancing opposite the window, caught a resident of the house watching them and cursed him. Needless to say, many a wide-eyed child has run past this house on a cold, dark night.

The real reason the window was black is because of the Doric style of the house. Immediately behind the window is a dividing wall, causing the window to appear black. The house is haunted, though, but not by the spirit of anyone who hanged himself. People have seen an apparition in white. Doors do open and close by themselves, and a former occupant found himself nervous many times when he was working late at night.

Queen Elizabeth II Health Sciences Centre

When the new Halifax Infirmary, a part of the QEII Health Sciences Centre, was built in 1994-95, excavators dug up old graves as they put in the foundations. Strange noises have been reported and rumour has it that it is an old Mi'kmaq burial ground or military cemetery from the days when the area, called Camp Hill, was a barracks. There are also rumours that strange shapes have been seen in the basement as well as vague stories about the fourth floor. Some people feel strange and get weird vibrations on that floor.

Richmond Street School

This school now houses the Family Court and is located on Devonshire Avenue. It is haunted by a ghost called Peggy. The school was severely damaged during the Halifax Explosion of 1917, so perhaps Peggy comes to us from those times.

The Bill Lynch Fair Curse

All Nova Scotians know about the annual Bill Lynch Fair, which comes to Halifax each May. According to legend, an employee of the fair slept with a Mi'kmaq woman, either a chief's wife or daughter. Needless to say, this angered the chief, and as he watched the two lovers escape in a boat, he cursed them and the fair for all time. He warned that foul weather would follow them wherever they went, and so it is that every May in Halifax when the fair comes to town, rain is sure to follow.

Halifax Shopping Centre

Most people wouldn't associate a shopping centre with ghosts and the unknown, but there are enough stories about this one to make a person pause before working there after hours. I worked here in my teens and was aware of the catacombs, as I liked to call them. Underneath all the stores were storage spaces allotted to each store and made up of metal fencing material so that you could see into and through each space. Naturally, it was quite dark and the shadows cast by the assorted boxes and garbage down there made it an eerie place.

Though I do not work at the mall anymore, I live just five minutes away and I still have friends who work there. They tell me of two ghosts that haunt the mall, one of which so upsets staff and security that it affects their job. The first haunting occurs down in my beloved catacombs. Sadly, one night after work a young man who worked at one of the stores above decided his life was no longer worth living and committed suicide. Since then employees report hearing the sounds of someone moving around one of the stalls, but no one can be found. At other times, the sounds of gentle weeping can be heard, but there is no one to be seen.

The second story really disturbs the security staff at the mall. Apparently, one day a workman was servicing the elevator shaft of Tower Two. The work was being done at night because Tower Two contains government offices and is the busiest tower in the mall. Work was proceeding normally this particular night when something went wrong and the man, who was working at the top of the elevator shaft, fell to his death. Since that time, the elevator has seemed to have a mind of its own at night. The door opens and closes without human input and the elevator often rises to the top of the tower for no known reason. Strange noises, like that of someone working inside the shaft, can be heard.

Old Ashburn Golf Course

This golf course can easily be seen by drivers as they come and go on the Bicentennial Highway. What is more rarely seen is the resident ghostly woman in the trees. She has been seen since the middle of the nineteenth century, and there are a couple of legends about who she was and why she haunts the golf course.

The first legend has it she was a local resident who was getting very old and wandered around in an advanced state of dementia. One day she disappeared and was found hanging from a tree just off one of the holes.

The second legend contends that an old man used to live on the grounds in a shack. When he died and the shack was torn down, workmen found the grave of an old woman. No matter which legend is right, when you pass this way or play at the course, look for a tall, thin, old woman who haunts the treeline.

2776 Dutch Village Road

This wonderful old house was once known as Rockwood Place, but is better known now as Eagan House and is owned by Halifax Regional Municipality. Though used for the modern purposes of a busy city, the house holds ancient ghosts. From the second floor come reports of a female ghost who appears in her wedding dress and wanders back and forth aimlessly, maybe searching for her lost love. Legend has it she was killed on her wedding day and that her bedroom was on the second floor, so she is often seen getting ready for a wedding that can never occur.

Purcell's Cove Road

This story came to me from a former resident who is a respected policeman and not someone I would accuse of having an overactive imagination. For a time in the 1980s he lived on

Purcell's Cove Road, across from the boat yard, just past Keefe Road.

This particular night Paul was taking out the garbage when he saw a woman with a long brown overcoat and scarf walking along the road in front of his house. When he reached the end of his driveway, an interval of only seven to ten seconds, the woman had vanished. Looking next door, he did not see her anywhere, and his neighbours were not home. Shrugging it off, he forgot about it, until he heard other area residents telling similar stories.

Interestingly enough, a short time after Paul told me this story, I happened to be speaking to a Halifax City Field employee and casually mentioned the Brown Lady. Though now a supervisor, this man had been a snowplow operator in the early 1980s. Coming down Purcell's Cove Road one evening plowing the newly fallen snow, he noticed a woman walking along the side of the road up ahead. Keeping an eye on her, he edged out away from her as he passed, but she fell or jumped in front of the vehicle.

Sick with worry and shock, he stopped the plow, jumped out of the cab and went back to see if she was dead or alive. Finding no one there after a lengthy search, he resumed his work but soon talked with other snowplow operators and heard the story. Apparently, a woman dressed in a brown coat and scarf was killed by a car one evening while she was out walking along the Purcell's Cove Road. Her spirit keeps trying to get to her destination, but never makes it.

Deadman's Island

For many years the history of Deadman and Melville Islands and their connection with the War of 1812 has gone unnoticed, but both the tangible and intangible residue of that time haunts us still.

American prisoners from that war were housed on these two islands and the prison can still be seen tucked away, almost hidden behind the sailboats at the Armdale Yacht Club on

Melville Island. Many prisoners died during their incarceration and were buried on Deadman's Island. Since then, developers, hikers, boaters and city maintenance workers have all discovered bones and skulls as the ground slowly gives up its dead. Naturally, the dead are said to be uneasy in their graves far from home and stories are told of strange sounds, mournful moans, and mysterious shadows on the island after dark.

Mount St. Vincent University

Some of the best times of my life occurred at the Mount, but I was unaware that any part of it was supposed to be haunted. It is said that the second floor of Evaristus Hall is haunted by ghostly footsteps that never approach or recede, but always sound about twenty feet away.

Prince's Lodge

In the early years of Halifax there came to these shores Prince Edward, Duke of Kent, later to become the father of Queen Victoria. He made his home on the edge of Bedford Basin with a grand mansion, heart-shaped pond, long trails through the woods, and a beautiful rotunda, called the Round House. The Prince was not without company. He had a French mistress, Julie de St. Laurent, and it was for her that the heart-shaped pond and rotunda were built. In later years Edward was forced to give up Julie when he had to marry to produce an heir, but for a few years there were many romantic nights by the shore in Halifax. However, there is a darker side of the story.

The Prince and Julie entertained often, and during one of these soirées a Colonel Olgilvie and a Captain Howard got into a heated argument. This led to a duel early one morning after the party, even though the Prince had forbidden such activity. Both men died of their wounds, and the Prince was not amused. He ordered that the body of Colonel Olgilvie be buried were it fell, just below the beautiful Round House. They say that the ghost of the dead colonel still wanders the grounds of the Round House, and will continue to do so until he has had a proper burial.

Birch Cove

Many years ago before Birch Cove became just another part of Halifax, there was an old rambling house where evil deeds were said to have been committed. No one knows for sure, but legend has it at least one woman was tortured in the house. Since that time, the spectre of a large black dog has been seen walking out of the woods and crossing the road before disappearing. I always look around when passing through Birch Cove but have yet to lay eyes on the spectral hound.

Bedford/Sackville/Beaver Bank/Waverley

These areas have long been seen as the suburbs of Halifax/ Dartmouth and are primarily residential. Some of the following stories can be found in *Cries at Kinsac Corner and Other Legends*, written by the students of a grade nine class at Sackville Heights Junior High in the 1970s.

Bedford Basin

As you travel along the scenic Bedford Highway between Halifax and Bedford, stop and roll your window down, and you may hear the sounds of muffled oars and straining men as they spend eternity trying to get ashore.

Fultz House Museum

This 138-year-old house at the corner of Sackville Drive and Cobequid Road was, for most of its history, the unremarkable residence of Bennett Fultz and his wife, Mary. Now it is a museum maintained by the Fultz Corner Restoration Society and the scene of an ongoing haunting.

For years, the staff at the Petro Canada gas station across the street have reported that lights come on at the museum late at night after all the staff have gone for the day. This occurs most often after midnight and has been reported for over twenty-five years. The electrical system has been checked out, but no obvious problems have been found to account for the lights to come on by themselves.

Footsteps have been heard on the hardwood floors late in the day after all visitors have left, prompting staff to search for intruders, but finding none. Once, one of the members of the Restoration Society was working alone in his office when he heard the back door open, then close, followed by the sounds of footsteps walking down the hall leading to the stairs to the second floor. Calling out and receiving no answer, he went in search of the culprit, but found he was alone in the old building.

No one is sure of the identity of the ghostly intruder, but Mary Fultz acted as a nurse for the community and many people died in the Fultz House over the years. Perhaps one of these unfortunate souls still prowls the place, or maybe it is Mary herself, endlessly walking the hall in search of someone to help.

Hillside Avenue, Lower Sackville

About forty years ago a man murdered his family in a fit of despair over losing his job and being unable to find any new work. On a dark, foggy night he stabbed his wife, infant daughter and dog, then buried them in a couple of holes he dug in the backyard. He then hung himself from a large elm tree. It is said that on foggy nights you can hear ghostly barking and see the body of the man slowly swinging from the elm tree.

Lily Lake

Every May 1, locals from Bedford gather along this small lake looking for the ghost of Mary, the fiancée of a young man named Henry. Almost two hundred years ago, during a spring picnic at the lake, young Mary went out in a canoe with two others to pick lilies. Reaching for one of the flowers, she lost her balance and fell in, quickly pulled down to the bottom by her heavy clothes. Her body was recovered later, but this sad event forever marked Henry, who would return to the lake from time to time to grieve his loss. A week before his final release from the pain of this world, many years after her drowning, Henry was at the lake late in the evening and saw the ghost of a smiling Mary gliding over the water, bathed in a beautiful glow, and accompanied by spectral music. She glided across the lake and disappeared into the woods, a forerunner of their reunion in death.

Maroon Hill

Today on Maroon Hill stands Beacon House, a second-hand clothing store. Originally, Beacon House was the Sackville Central School and began as a school for Black children. Local legend has it that the school was built on land owned by a reclusive lady, who left instructions in her will that a school be built for Black children only on her land. This was done, but with the passage of time it became necessary for white children to attend the school. This apparently did not sit well with the spirit of the lady benefactor. She reportedly manifested writing on the wall and a pair of ghostly hands that were seen floating in space. She must have gotten used to the idea of white children attending the school, though, since there have been no recent expressions of her displeasure. However, local residents still believe the building is haunted.

Windsor Highway/Jubilee Lane

The intersection of the Number 1 Highway, known as the Windsor Highway, and Jubilee Lane is the reported resting place of a woman whose husband loved her so much he buried her on their property which bordered the road. There have been reports of groaning and even sightings of a mysterious light seen nearby.

Gulliver's Lane

Gulliver's Lane used to branch off the Lucasville Road just before it reaches the Number 1 Highway at Middle Sackville. During World War One, a man named Gulliver was called up to serve, but instead he hung himself from a large tree beside the lane. For many years people reported seeing his body hanging from the tree at night, but it would be gone by daylight. The lane was abandoned shortly thereafter. Some part of the lane might still be visible under the trees behind the newer houses on the Lucasville Road. The stump of the tree may even still be there for the brave to visit on a dark night.

Springfield Lake

During the night you might see a light gliding across the lake. If you are unfortunate enough to get close to the light, you will see that it is the ghost of a woman who was murdered many years ago by her husband, who threw her from their boat in the middle of the lake. Her ghost still keeps watch, hoping one day to find her husband and exact revenge for her murder.

There is another ghostly woman who reportedly haunts this lake. She is looking for her fiancé, not in anger but in grief. Apparently, he drowned in the lake before their wedding day and she died of grief over her loss. She is now said to glide across the lake in her wedding gown, drenched in blood and carrying a lantern as she endlessly searches for him.

Lewis Lake

There is a legend that a cabin once stood near Lewis Lake in Upper Sackville and that anyone who occupied the cabin was treated to a visit by the ghost of an old lady called The Lady of the Lake. Apparently, she would materialize in front of the alarmed owners. In one case she was said to have written a message on the wall, instructing the occupants to leave.

Kinsac

They used to hang criminals here at one time. There is a peculiar thing about the gallows that served this area: when it was no longer used it was still left in place, perhaps out of laziness or maybe to serve as a silent warning. The last life it took was that of a young boy. He had gone missing and the search party found him hanging from the gallows, blowing in the wind. Whether it was an accident, suicide, or murder, no one ever determined. But shortly after his death, moans and crying could be heard from the area of the old gallows. Then a "white shadow" approximately the size of the little boy could be seen against the gallows. Finally, authorities took down the gallows and the crying and moaning stopped, but there are still reports of a little "white shadow" in the woods here.

One of the most terrifying legends in Nova Scotia comes from this area. The Kinsac Creature, part dog and part wolf, with long white hair and glowing red eyes, prowls these parts.

Beaver Bank

Reportedly, from the Rawdon Road northeasterly through the woods to Enfield runs a series of tracks that local legend has dubbed "the Devil's Footprints." They are said to have been left by the Devil as he walked through the woods carrying a bag of gold. The tracks run up to one side of Grand Lake, then resume on the other side as if the maker just walked on or under the lake. Many people have searched for the "gold" that the Devil brought with him, but so far they haven't been successful.

Maritimers may be aware of the Richibucto Spectre in New Brunswick, a woman in white who chases cars along Highway 134, but not many know about the Flying Spectre of Beaver Bank. Travelling north on the Beaver Bank Road, known as Highway 354, about ten minutes after passing Kinsac, you begin a steep ascent into the hilly backbone of Nova Scotia. Just before you come to Beaver Bank Villa on a straight stretch of road, keep your eyes peeled at night for "The Phantom," as some call it. This figure is dressed in a long white cape and floats over the road at night, with only its intensely red eyes visible to frightened drivers.

Blue Pond

It might be a little difficult to get to this location since this pond is reported to be deep in the woods north of Beaver Bank. However, it has been thirty years since the legend was written down, so the pond may be more accessible now that the area is more developed.

Local legend has it there is a pond in Beaver Bank with water so blue that it gave the pond its name. It seems a strange egg was found one day and it continued to grow larger and larger until it was dumped into the pond. From that egg emerged a "large, scaly, green serpent or dragon." This dragon is still said to haunt the pond and carry off the unwary visitor.

Windsor Junction

Approximately every twenty-five years reports emerge of a mysterious phantom feline coming from the woods around the railway tracks here. A shiny, pitch-black panther is sighted along the tracks and disappears into the woods at the approach of any human. Its estimated weight is sixty-five pounds and it follows the tracks towards Beaver Bank.

Cobequid Road Railway Crossing

Many years ago children were playing near this railway crossing when they noticed a strange lady walking along the tracks. An approaching train caught their attention and by the time they looked back towards the woman, she had disappeared – although she had been out of the children's sight for only a few seconds. Returning home later that day, the children told their parents of what they had seen.

By the children's description of the woman, the parents were able to determine she was someone who had died a few years previously. Her husband worked for the railway company at the time. The next day, he was killed by a train at the same spot where the children had seen his ghostly wife twenty-four hours before. Though this series of events happened many years ago, reports still come in of a woman appearing just before the approach of a train and vanishing as it passes.

Miller's Lake

This story comes to us from Miller's Lake. A railwayman lost his right arm to a train one day and then turned into a bitter recluse. Few people ever saw him, but over the years various people would disappear and never be found. When some hikers happened upon the recluse's cabin one day, they were horrified to find the right arms of several people, but no recluse. When the authorities arrived, they found the evidence as well as signs that the recluse had fled with a few belongings and a blue lantern. From that time onward, stories would be told of a mysterious blue light seen along the lake and up the mountain alongside it.

Waverley Road

Throughout the United States and Canada there is an urban legend about a phantom hitchhiker who is picked up by an unknowing good samaritan and given instructions as to where he or she wishes to be dropped off. Some versions say the hitchhiker gets out at a cemetery, others say at a house, and still others say that the hitchhiker disappears from the backseat of the car. When the driver goes to the door of the house mentioned by his ghostly guest, he is informed that he or she died many years ago and is still trying to get home. Although this legend is mostly just that, it seems to have originated in the 1930s in Arkansas.

Nova Scotia has its version of this legend, which takes place on the Waverley Road. It differs from the urban legend only in that it is the good samaritan who is the ghost.

The story goes that the ghost of a truck driver named Joe Santos still drives his truck, called the Phantom 309, along the Waverley Road. Joe was killed in Phantom 309 in an accident many years ago. In the mid-1960s, reports surfaced that people were picked up by this man who identified himself as Joe Santos. Later these hitchhikers were to learn that the man they accepted a drive from had been dead some years.

Dutch Settlement

The Dutch Settlement Elementary School is haunted by a quiet ghost who spends most of his time silently watching staff and students going about their business. Sometimes you can feel a cold draft of air as he passes you. Apparently, he spends most of his time in the gym. At night when the rest of the school is quiet and only a janitor or late-working staff member is around, they can hear the soft sobbing of a lonely ghost.

Dartmouth

Devil's Island

This island at the mouth of the harbour has long had some disturbing stories associated with it. Strange fires, ghostly footsteps and visitations from the Devil all abound here. Though abandoned now, for many years there were year-round residents on the island and was a favourite place to visit and picnic for Nova Scotia's dean of folklore, Helen Creighton.

Popular lore states that Devil's Island got its name from an incident that happened to one Casper Henneberry during a party late one night. Henneberry went outside for a moment and when he returned he was as white as a ghost. Upon being questioned, he stated that he saw the Devil outside against the house. Even stranger was that the Devil was in the form of a halibut. Obviously, his friends laughed at that, but the next day they found Henneberry leaning over the side of his boat, drowned. Since that day the island has been known as Devil's Island.

Perhaps more horrifying, legend has it a resident of Devil's Island was found decapitated one morning after he too apparently met the Devil. The island is also reputed to have buried treasure at various locations. Some say it rests in a bottomless pit much like Oak Island's fabled treasure. Others say it was in a lake in the middle of the island, but that lake was drained and nothing was found. If there is any treasure on the island, it would likely be pirate or French treasure and secreted there before 1749 when Halifax was established.

McNab's Island

McNab's Island is one of the last areas of almost unspoiled beauty in Halifax. It has been used as a place to hang pirates, to defend the city with its fortifications, and to welcome residents for an afternoon of hiking or picnicking.

The name comes from Peter McNab, who once owned the island. He is said to still be there. Upon his death, he was buried on the island he loved so much, but legend has it his body was buried on one end of the island, with his head interred on the opposite end. To this day his spirit is seen walking the length of the island looking to reclaim his head.

Peter McNab IV was a witness to the sea serpent said to live off the harbour approaches. In 1853, he watched a twenty-foot, eel-like animal with a small head moving in an undulating motion off Ives Point at the northwestern tip of the island.

There was once an orphanage on McNab's, which one night burned down, caused by a candle that got too close to a curtain. Many children were injured or killed, and their anguished and frightened cries are said to echo throughout the island. Reports also come down to us of a floating candle seen near the ruins of the orphanage.

There are also reports of a ghostly horse and carriage heard making its way across the island on one of the lonely roads.

As with Devil's Island, McNab's supposedly is the repository for treasure. French fishermen are said to have buried their treasure at McNab's Cove in the middle of the island. An old French gold mine is thought by some to have existed here before the founding of Halifax, and strange men with tools for searching and digging have been seen on the island.

Treasure reportedly at the north end of the island comes from an unlikely source. Bill Lynch, he of the cursed fair, was believed to have stashed a large quantity of silver and gold coins. Apparently, for five years in a row he had four-foot-long copper tubes constructed in Halifax and some believe he stored his coins in these tubes. His sister would meet him on the island and they would bury this money every September. This was a dangerous practice, for McNab's was inhabited at the time, but if the story is true, no one must have seen them for the treasure is said to still be there.

Not all the terrors are on land. The waters surrounding the island can be treacherous too. More than one ship has sailed out into the fog around McNab's Island and disappeared. This story was given to me by Jamie Cox, whose friend regularly went to the island. One time the friend's brother was waiting in the boat as it was tied up at the dock. He was startled by sounds of something scraping the length of the boat's hull. Needless to say, he quickly vacated the boat. Much later, when they brought it up onto a dock in Halifax, they saw the keel had been scraped as if by claws.

Nova Scotia Hospital

For many years the Nova Scotia Hospital has been a mental institution and the older buildings on the site looked cold and forbidding, like a fortress or prison. So perhaps it isn't surprising that such an atmosphere would generate at least one ghost.

One of my students in the 1990s had worked on the fifth floor of the hospital and it wasn't long before she was initiated into the secret. The wards were kept securely locked and staff had to let visitors in. It was only her second or third night when she looked over her shoulder and saw the door open. Thinking someone hadn't properly closed it and not wanting to make a fuss since she was new, she got up and closed it again. A little while later she heard a knock on the door and when she went to see who it was, no one was there. No sooner had she sat back down and begun her work when the knock came once more. Again, no one was there when she went to the door.

At this point, a colleague came to the desk and she mentioned the peculiar occurrences. The co-worker sighed, gave her a sad smile and told her to get used to it. The floor had a ghost. Hospital staff did not know who the spirit was, but whoever it was, it liked to play tricks – but only on the fifth floor and only at night. Soon the knocks and occasional open door became second nature and nothing to be much remarked upon.

Dartmouth Shore

There are legends of buried treasure somewhere along the Dartmouth shore. Surprisingly, the treasure is said to be Spanish in origin, not the usual culprits: the French, English or pirates.

One night many years ago three men decided to dig for the treasure, probably somewhere between Tufts Cove and the Defence Research Establishment Atlantic. As they dug deep for the gold, they heard a ship weigh anchor just off shore. They recognized it as a Spanish ship, and this was quickly confirmed when a small boat with pirates began to row towards them. Seeing the pirates outnumbered them, as well as being considerably better armed with guns and swords versus the shovels and picks of the diggers, the men beat a hasty retreat.

They never went back to the shore to see if the pirates took back their gold, or whether the whole thing was a ghostly re-enactment of the original burial. In that case, the treasure may still lie somewhere along the rocky shore.

95 King Street

Although no confirmed ghosts reside here, there are a couple of mysteries connected with it. The house was owned in the mid-1800s by Dr. John MacDonald, Governor of Dalhousie College and a Justice of the Peace. He was also a respected businessman, so it was a surprise in 1846 when he vanished off the face of the earth. There have never been any concrete leads as to where he went, although foul play was most likely the reason for his disappearance. In 1879, there was a skull found buried under the basement of the house. Popular legend had it that the skull belonged to one of the *Saladin* pirates who were hanged in 1844. Perhaps if modern DNA testing had been available, it would have been discovered that the skull was that of Dr. MacDonald, the former owner of the house.

18 Octerloney Street

This lovely old house was occupied for many years by a pair of elderly women, a bastion of sedate nobility in a rapidly modernizing neighbourhood. Both of the ladies have since died and the house is now the home of a distinguished law office. But maybe the women haven't left their old home behind, for strange noises are often reported in the house. There is also the frequent appearance of a person in a window when the house is empty.

Cole Harbour

According to the Fort Wayne, Indiana, *Weekly Gazette* of April 14, 1892, Cole Harbour residents were "much excited and terrified" by a "gorilla" (Bigfoot) that was sighted in the woods here. The creature was seen to be seven feet high.

Eastern Shore

Grey Ladies of the Eastern Shore

If the Annapolis Valley is the home of wandering Women in White, then the Eastern Shore is home to the Grey Ladies. Whereas the spectres of the Valley wander aimlessly, the Grey Ladies along the Eastern Shore appear to warn fishermen and unwary travellers of peril ahead. Seen as a certain sign of impending doom, the Grey Lady is thus the most feared of all spirits in this book. Before a storm or calamity she appears in a grey haze, gliding noiselessly across the water, her head hidden by a dark veil or, as some more imaginative souls believe, without a head at all. Speculation abounds as to her origins, but most believe she was the unfortunate victim of a shipwreck somewhere along the shore and seeks to warn those who are in peril of sharing her fate.

Seaforth

The first Grey Lady can be found here at Seaforth. If you nicely ask one of the locals, they may tell you in which house the Grey Lady floats down the staircase to greet her guests.

Middle Musquodoboit

Years ago a local man named Ike made a joke about the Devil that he has an eternity to regret. One day he and his friends returned from a particular stream that had a large rock in the middle of it, impeding the progress of anyone travelling down it. Always a man with a colourful metaphor, Ike swore that if the Devil would only move that rock he would be much obliged. Beginning that night and for the next two nights the man heard his name being called from somewhere down by the stream, but he wouldn't go. The next day Ike and his friends went down to the stream and the rock had vanished. The stream was clear. Even though Ike hadn't participated in the exercise he was afraid of what would happen, and shortly thereafter while walking on the ice near that spot, he fell through and was drowned. The Devil had his revenge.

Caribou Mines

"The Beast" is said to prowl the woods near the gold mines here. No one has seen it, but its strange high-pitched cries, often compared to the scream of a woman in agony, are frequently heard, especially at night. Some wonder if the digging many years ago at one of the gold mines has unleashed a creature from the deep bowels of the earth.

East Petpeswick

The spectre of a Grey Lady wandering the shore here is supposed to be connected with buried treasure. The unusual thing about this phantom is that she is often seen carrying a pair of stockings in her hand. If you get to watch her long enough, you may even see her stop, sit down upon a rock and put them on. I wonder if anyone has thought to check under that rock?

A ghostly man-o-war can be seen sailing up the Petpeswick Inlet on moonlit nights in search of its earthly treasure cached somewhere around here hundreds of years ago.

Petpeswick Inlet

From here comes a story of a Norwegian barque that is sighted before a storm. The vessel lost her way during a gale and ran onto the rocky shore. Sometimes the vision appears as the ship, while at other times it is just a ball of light, described as shining like a big star. Like the ship we will meet in Pleasant

Harbour, this ghost ship comes into the harbour and disappears into the woods on shore.

Kent Island

The lighthouse here is said to be haunted by the great British admiral Horatio Nelson.

Jeddore Harbour

Another mysterious ghost ship is seen here. It appears most often on calm nights though its sails are full with unearthly wind as it moves silently across the water. Sometimes it sails up the channel to the Salmon River before turning and sailing back out into the Atlantic. Excited voices speaking in a foreign language at times are heard coming across the water from the eerie ghost ship.

Ashore at Myers Point appears the spectre of a sailor, dressed in a blue suit with brass buttons and bib cap, walking aimlessly about. There are also sightings of a headless woman, dressed in white, who supposedly knows the whereabouts of buried treasure. No one has followed her long enough to find out. Observers could also follow yet another wandering soul, this time dressed all in grey with a grey hat, which shimmers in the moonlight.

Salmon River

Your trip over the Salmon River Bridge can be a frightening experience and one that foretells tragedy, so keep you windows up and the radio or CD blaring. Though no one knows why, when some travel over the bridge, they can hear the sound of people rowing a boat. Looking out towards the harbour they then can see two men rowing for a few seconds before mysteriously vanishing before their unbelieving eyes. Shortly afterwards, notice of a death will come to those who have seen this terrifying forerunner.

Ship Harbour

On one of the islands near the mouth of Ship Harbour rests a fortune in pirate treasure. It consists of coin and bullion and was buried in wooden casks, which of course would have rotted by now. The treasure allegedly rests in a gully on the island with two feet of dirt over it.

Number 7 Highway

The Number 7 Highway between Ship Harbour and East Ship Harbour is said to be haunted by the ghost of a woman in a wedding dress. Legend has it a mother and daughter were on their way to the daughter's wedding and had a car accident. The bride-to-be was killed. Now her ghost can be seen walking slowly along the road in her crumpled and bloody wedding dress.

Goose Island

Goose Island is small, only two hundred metres long and one hundred metres wide, flat and windswept. Though small and uninviting, this island does have its share of mystery. The sounds of a boat rowing by are often heard, but none is found upon investigation. It is believed that pirate gold is buried somewhere on the island, and strange markings are carved into the cliff on the eastern end. Once, the shattering of dozens of bottles was heard coming from the cliff on the western side of the island and since that day it is thought the treasure must be buried there. Finally, a strange woman in grey has been seen walking on Goose Island even though she couldn't possibly be there.

Pleasant Harbour

From here comes yet another phantom ship legend of the Eastern Shore. On clear moonlit nights it sails into Pleasant Harbour and can be heard dropping anchor. Unlike many ghost ships, this one is fully manned and observers can hear the crew moving about on the ship, talking in some strange language, and working on some unseen job. At times, the ship forgoes dropping anchor and sails right up to the shore and disappears into the woods. This has led some to believe the phantom ship is connected with treasure buried somewhere on the shore.

Mushaboom

This phantom ship sighting has a twist on it. In winter, a fully rigged sailing ship can be seen coming down the harbour, even when it is frozen over, and the sound of the anchor being dropped can be heard for miles around. Sometimes the ship comes down the harbour as a ball of fire, reinforcing the relationship between ghost ships and unearthly fire.

Sheet Harbour

Before you reach the town of Sheet Harbour, the road curves around the actual harbour. As you drive, remember the legend that somewhere along the road across from the town a section is known as the Ghost Road. Back in 1899, locals would hear the wails of the dead, and some saw coffins and human shapes along the road.

Sable Island

It is unlikely you will actually be able to go out to Sable Island, unless you happen to be in the gas and oil industry. The island is about a hundred miles off the coast of Nova Scotia, and is pretty much left to itself, except for the odd gas exploration vessel passing by. A few hundred years ago the story was very different. Sable Island was given the name "Graveyard of the Atlantic" because of all the ships that were wrecked upon its shores. The treacherous currents, coupled with dense fogs and the unpredictable weather of the North Atlantic, served to dash many a captain's hopes and many lives. Needless to say, with all this death and destruction there are a couple of resident ghosts on the island.

The first ghost concerns the vision of a woman who is missing a finger. Mrs. Copeland was a passenger on the ship *Frances*, which went down in 1799. The *Frances* was an important ship with many upper-class passengers and much valuable cargo. There is some dispute as to whether the lady was murdered or not. Not disputed, however, is that one of Mrs. Copeland's fingers was cut off to get at a gold ring. Her body was buried in a nearby graveyard along with other poor unfortunates from the *Frances*. Soon, stories began to circulate around the island of the apparition of a woman with a mutilated hand walking the shore where the bodies had washed in.

One of the beaches of Sable Island was known as Haunted Beach when the island was inhabited. For many years the bodies of ill-fated souls from the various shipwrecks would appear on this beach, but it was one body in particular that spawned the name. One morning after a vicious storm, residents were walking along the beach looking for anything that washed ashore and came across many bodies. One was that of a young mother who was still clasping her child in her arms. Upon closer inspection it was found that the baby was still alive. It only lived for a short time and was buried on the island, but separate from its mother. For years afterward, residents would tell of pitiful cries coming from the beach and the apparition of a wailing woman appearing on dark, foggy nights, endlessly searching for her child.

Guysborough County

Port Bickerton

The lighthouse at Barachois Head is automated now, as are most lighthouses across the country. Something romantic has been lost with automation, for lighthouse keepers were also keepers of local folklore and tellers of mystery.

The keepers of the Barachois Head lighthouse were more than tellers of mystery in the 1950s; they experienced it first-hand. Lights began to appear along the beach as if someone was walking through the cold, dark night with a lantern. But a visitor never appeared. Later, the lighthouse light would go out or dim for no reason. Upon investigation it would appear someone had climbed up, opened the hatch, and interfered with the light, but as with the light on the beach, no evidence of anyone being present was ever found. There were no tracks, no tire marks nor the sounds of anyone but the two keepers.

Little Harbour

The British troopship *Billow* sank in a snowstorm in 1830. It struck a reef off Ram Island with the loss of all aboard. It is said that observers could hear the ship's band playing as it sank. To this day the residents of Little Harbour say that when the wind blows hard in a storm, you can still hear the ship's band playing "The Gay Cockade"as it did that fateful night.

Strait of Canso

Somewhere along the Strait is Nova Scotia's only merman. I have heard these stories from a few different places, so it may be more than a fish story. There is no word on any female company for him yet.

Pirate Harbour

Another Captain Kidd fable comes out of this little harbour on the Strait of Canso. Kidd reportedly spent one winter around here in order to escape capture by British warships. As usual, Kidd was unsuccessful in evading his pursuers and took the time to stop and bury his ill-gotten goods. This legend was given a macabre twist, one common with ordinary pirate treasure, but rare for any associated with Kidd. Supposedly, a Black man named Black Peter was murdered in order to guard the treasure. It is said his headless ghost walks the shoreline between MacGuire's Gulch and Susie's Island looking for his head. He is also seen wandering along the brook that bears his name, Black Peter's Brook.

Richmond County

Port Hawkesbury

Two haunted houses can be found in Port Hawkesbury. On Philpott Street there is a house that is haunted by hallway lights coming on and off. Musty smells alternate with the smell of sulphur or sweet perfume. Locals know the second house for its cold spots and the spectres of a mother and her child.

Port Malcolm Bay

Back in the age of sail, a fully rigged ship sank in a storm and many bodies were discovered washed up on shore. One of them was the captain, who was said to have a small child clutched in his cold, dead arms. To this day, when the wind blows from the southeast, you can hear the screams of victims.

Glasgow Point

There is an apparition of a headless skater, wearing a long flowing gown, that haunts this area. It has been seen skating quickly before disappearing into an opening in the ice. The ghost is believed to be one of two girls who were drowned here one winter day.

There are also reports of strange balls of light sighted on cold, dark nights in this area. This *feu follet* once stopped a man and wouldn't let him pass until morning.

Gros Nez Island

Stories are still told of a light that can be seen in any weather, far off in the distance on Gros Nez Island. It looks like the small light of a rowboat, but no boat is ever seen. The light appears and disappears with no regular pattern or apparent cause. The tales originated before the time of electricity and though not as frequent now, some say the light still shines in the lonely distance from time to time.

Point Michaud

In 1745, the French frigate *St. Michel*, loaded with gold and silver, was on its way to the great French fortress of Louisbourg. The ship was almost caught up in the battle raging between the British and French over Louisbourg, but luck was with it and the vessel escaped, only to run aground off Point Michaud. There was never any official attempt at salvaging the wreck, so a vast fortune still lies somewhere offshore. However, before you get excited and go diving for the treasure, be forewarned that there were sightings of a soldier standing guard near the wreck. Some people believed he was an apparition of one of those who died, and is still doing his duty.

The Black Ground

The Black Ground is an uninhabited wide open space, with the ruins of old foundations, ancient paths and alders, shrubs and overgrowth. It is bordered by a lake and tall spruces, and a dirt road cuts through it. No one seems able to live there for very long, and out of the dense overgrowth come piercing cries of unseen birds of prey. Strange grunts from unknown animals and other unsettling sounds emanate from it.

Human shapes appear out of nowhere. One time three old hunchbacked women, dressed in black with shawls over their heads, passed through and disappeared into the woods, heedless of all attempts to intercept them. In long ago days when there were houses atop the now crumbling foundations, ghostly figures of faces and people would be seen inside the houses, accompanied by the noises of falling boards. Other stories tell of "beastly utterances."

There are rumours of hidden treasure and maybe that is what those mysterious apparitions are searching for. But what is causing those horrible sounds?

French Cove

It is here the sailors of a British ship are said to have buried gold that was to be used for paying soldiers. It seems there were too many French troops around so the British officers thought that burying the gold would be the wisest course of action. They were right because just after they buried the gold, they were attacked by pirates who destroyed the ship, killing all aboard. Since that time many have wandered the area looking for signs of the treasure, but so far none have been found.

Cape Breton Regional Municipality

Louisbourg

At its heyday, Louisbourg was France's greatest fortress in the New World. It was certainly the greatest threat to the British Empire, so Britain launched two major battles to conquer the fortress. Both times the British won, but after the first battle, they ceded the fort back to the French. During these seesaw times many ships were wrecked either in the harbour or in its approaches. Over the years some of these wrecks have been found, and some money and treasure recovered, but there is likely much more to be had.

Also at Louisbourg walks the ghost of Captain Robert Duhaget (1702-1757). Duhaget served at Louisbourg and Port Toulouse (St. Peter's) and there are no records of his meeting an untimely death. However, he has been seen by many employees of the national park in the house that bears his name. He has been observed haunting the attic of Duhaget House in full French military dress, as well as walking the grounds of the fortress, and even praying in the chapel each evening. No one knows what he may be praying for, but one hopes he soon finds the absolution he seeks.

Scatarie Island

This large island was one of many small settlements that surrounded the French Fortress of Louisbourg. After the last battle for Louisbourg when the British finally took complete possession of Nova Scotia, the French inhabitants of Scatarie Island were forced to leave. Today the residents of Scatarie Island report that not all those early inhabitants have left. Some still remain, or at least their spirits do. There have been many reports of strange occurrences: the ground shaking; shadows that were taken to be the dead walking the island; gold buried deep with skeletons on top to scare away looters; ghosts of dead mariners appearing two days before their deaths; gold and more gold, perhaps more gold buried or lost here than anywhere else in Nova Scotia.

Blackett's Lake

Strange stories come from around here and some people have noted that the area just "feels" wrong to them.

There is also a story told about a girl who lived in Ontario and took a plane to Sydney, then a taxi to Blackett's Lake. When she arrived at the lake she proceeded to drown herself, leaving no note to explain why. The most perplexing aspect to the story is that she did not know anyone in Cape Breton, nor had she been here before.

Other reports come to us that Coxheath Mountain, whose slopes lead to the lake, has peculiar geological properties, for many compasses will not function properly. Strange lights are seen over the lake and surrounding areas. Hearing terrible screams and the sense of being followed are common to those who dare to walk around here at night.

Sydney

One hot summer afternoon at the turn of the twentieth century a ship was becalmed in the harbour and its captain and crew witnessed a strange meteorological phenomenon. A weird cloud came towards the city and as it got within a quarter of a mile, they saw the images of "animals, birds and reptiles" in it. Those on board saw animals they had never seen before. Soon the cloud changed and the men beheld a battlefield scene. They couldn't recognize where or when the battle had taken place, but they could see Scottish soldiers fighting in their kilts. There was no sound, but the vision was bloody and full of carnage. The captain went ashore the next day and made inquiries, but apparently only he and his men had seen the magnificent sights.

Sydney Coal Mines

Stories abound about the coal mines and their ghosts. Back in the days when one mine was a going concern, it was haunted by the spectre of a horse and a pit boy who used to work there. The horse, named Spot, was quite intelligent and was always paired with a young boy named Sol. One day they were killed when a tunnel roof collapsed on them. The next day an inspector claimed to have seen their ghosts working as usual, but his story was laughed off. Until the next day. Every day for a whole year at nine o'clock exactly, the same hour they died, the ghosts of Sol and Spot would carry out their duties as they did in life. After the year was up, the spirits of Sol and his pit pony disappeared. The mine is closed now, but who knows what walks the abandoned shafts with no one to see them?

Other coal mines reported mysterious lights, some stationary, others moving as if attached to someone. No one was ever found, though, and the lights may still shine through the lonely closed shafts to this day.

Front Lake

This lake has the reputation of being a nice quiet place with a lovely beach. The lake itself is only a mile long and a half-mile wide, yet its peaceful surface hides a darker mystery, for in Front Lake there may be one of Nova Scotia's many sea serpents.

The first reports of something strange came from a family named Ferguson in 1820. They described a long, monstrous snake that was sleeping along the shore. Their appearance disturbed the creature, which promptly retreated into the water.

There were no more reports of the creature until around the turn of the twentieth century when one night two men in a boat saw it in the middle of the lake. Another witness was on the shore and confirmed their story. Other reports have come down through the years of something strange and hideous sleeping on the sandy shore, so be careful if you decide to stop for a suntan or swim here.

Cranberry Lake

For more than a hundred years, nearby residents have reported seeing a creature living in the lake. It is about twelve feet in length, dark, with a horse-like head. Some observers thought the animal was looking for something on the shore. A company was even formed once to hunt down the animal, but as they decided to try this in winter, it is not surprising they had no success.

Barrachois

This is a rare occurrence in Nova Scotia – a ghostly train. The only other report of a similar spectre is from somewhere in the Annapolis Valley, but I've never been able to pin down an exact location. A phantom train glides along non-existent tracks along St. Andrew's Channel towards the headlands of the Bras d'Or Lake.

Bras d'Or Lake

Local Mi'kmaq tell the legend of a lone phantom Indian who paddles his canoe up the lake just before a storm.

Victoria County

Boularderie

This story comes from Mary Fraser's *Folklore of Nova Scotia*. There is a "dark, deep gulch" here with a cliff that towers over it "ominously." Down in that deep gulch lies a gigantic rock that has an evil legend associated with it. The Devil was cheated out of a soul one night and took his anger out on the towering cliff. He heaved a boulder off the cliff and threw it into the gulch, where it can still be seen today.

Also, strange lights are reported to have been seen flying over Boularderie from time to time.

Kelly's Mountain

When the time came to put a new road through Kelly's Mountain, it had to be built through land belonging to an Irishman named Patty Kelly. Kelly was a drunkard, and moonshiner to boot. He should have been happy when his land was expropriated for the Transcanada Highway, for at least he would have had money for booze. But he wasn't then, and he is apparently not happy even now that he is dead.

This stretch of road, as the highway descends to the Bras d'Or Bridge, has seen more than its share of accidents. Some say that the ghost of Kelly is the cause of some of these accidents as he seeks revenge for being driven off his land.

In a tale reminiscent of the Hairy Hands of Devon in the United Kingdom, some people claim that an unseen force twists the steering wheel, causing them to drive off the road. At other times, motorists see Kelly standing in the middle of the road and then he runs right through the approaching car.

The area Kelly haunts most often is the east side of the mountain where there is a sharp curve in the road. It is here that he jumps out in front of traffic, hoping drivers will swerve to miss him and careen out of control off the side of the mountain.

Indian Brook

Somewhere between here and the North Shore are legends that Glooscap had a lodge in one of the caves that dot the shore opposite Bird Islands. This cave is also known as the Fairy Hole, and supposedly no one has ever reached the end of the cave. Some say these legends add further weight to the possibility that Henry Sinclair, Earl of Orkney, reached these shores, since we are pretty sure he reached Cape Breton.

Legend explains the presence of Bird Islands by saying that Glooscap was showing off for two maidens. When he jumped from his canoe, he broke it in two, and thus Bird Islands were born. The maidens were laughing at him and, being short-tempered, Glooscap turned them into stone. So if you want to search for the cave, you must first find the two stones that guard the entrance to it.

Ingonish

Ingonish is home to a couple of legends. First, buried treasure supposedly rests in this area. Also, Keltic Lodge, a popular resort, is haunted. The ghost of Henry Clay Corson has haunted the lodge off and on since it was built in 1952. He came to this place at the turn of the century with Alexander Graham Bell, who lived in Baddeck. Henry also liked the charms of rural Cape Breton and decided to make a home here.

Henry Clay Corson died, and in the 1930s the province expropriated the land from the rich industrialist's estate and built Keltic Lodge. Some employees feel he has returned to haunt the popular resort. They have observed doors open and close on their own, televisions come on for no reason, and, most hideously, a ghostly figure of someone from the knees down. There have also been sightings of a smiling old man that mysteriously disappears after walking through the lobby.

There is also the story that some people saw the ghost of Mrs. Corson the day of her death. Two boys walking along Middle Head, a narrow strip of land past Keltic Lodge, saw an old man walking towards them. Soon he was obscured by some trees and when they next saw him he had changed into a she. Now there was an old woman walking towards them, with no sign of anyone else near. Soon, even she disappeared, and the boys later found out that it was the very same day that Mrs. Corson died. It was then they realized they must have seen her spirit, perhaps taking a final walk around the place where she lived. But who was the first apparition the boys saw? Could it have been Mr. Corson?

Sugar Loaf

There is a fairy mound around here and if a brownie comes out and gives you some buttermilk, then you will be lucky the rest of your life.

Capstick

Our fourth Bigfoot story comes to us from the northernmost tip of Cape Breton. A man-like creature covered with long hair like a big fur coat, over eight feet tall, with arms that hang below the knees has been sighted from Capstick along the shore to Meat Cove, through the backwoods and ending up at Lowland Cove. An interesting difference from the usual Sasquatch sightings is that the creature's eyes are described as "beautiful." It first appeared many years ago when mining in the area apparently disturbed it and it began to venture near civilization. Hunters have reported seeing its tracks for years. They are manlike, yet huge and the stride is six or seven feet. The last reports of the creature come from the early 1990s.

Inverness County

Cheticamp Island

In the late 1800s, the island was home to several fish camps. Men lived ashore and commuted to and from the camps on the weekends. Two fishermen in particular were travelling back to the island Sunday night when they heard the hoofbeats of a galloping horse. Turning to see who it was, they were upset to see a stranger, clad wholly in white with a white cap and cape billowing behind him, on a white horse. The men saw the apparition many times, but no one else ever reported it.

St. Joseph Du Moine

From just down the shore from Cheticamp Island comes another story of the *feu follet*, or jack o'lantern. This blazing ball of light would appear late at night to lonely travellers, making a "low, siren-like hum," and either following them or hovering before them, blocking their way. A folk wisdom tells that in order to get rid of the *feu follet*, you must drive your knife into the nearest tree.

Margaree

There is a brook, called the Bochdan Brook, hereabouts that got its name from the wicked spirit, or *bochdan*, that haunts the area. The story goes that a drunkard died and was buried on an island in unconsecrated ground across the way from the brook and has chosen to haunt it in order to terrify the living.

Also, pirate treasure is widely believed to be buried along the shore opposite Margaree Island. Whenever someone is foolish enough to dig for it, a phantom ship appears and the ghosts of the long-dead pirates appear to frighten off the searchers. Once, the apparitions followed some searchers back to their home and surrounded the place until midnight, pressing their ghastly dead white faces up against the windows until the last toll of the midnight hour pulled them back to the land of the dead.

Inverness

According to Mary Fraser in *Folklore of Nova Scotia*, the whole area of Inverness used to be called the Shean, from the Gaelic *sithean*, which means "house of fairies." Belief in fairies and reports of their activities are common here because of the Celtic ancestry of the inhabitants. Many people have seen the little people and some refuse to walk alone at night. It is said that on a nearby hill the fairies used to gather in the thousands, disappearing suddenly when they discovered they were being watched.

Sight Point

Various animal manifestations haunt the area here. There is also a *bochdan* (hobgoblin) that scares people and animals crossing over a bridge, which is a very secluded and lonely place.

Lake Ainslie

This is a popular place for summer homes and cabins, but it is said that a sea serpent haunts this lake. Unlike most sightings of a sea monster, however, this one is described as looking like a whale with a couple of humps along its back.

Mabou

Ghostly birds and countless apparitions protect the pirate treasure hidden in a stream near Mabou. Treasure seekers have been molested by large flocks of black birds. One party noticed some men up the shore watching them, and before their eyes the group of men soon numbered in the thousands. They retreated home, and believe to this day that the birds they noticed flying overhead turned into the men, and they were the spirits summoned by the ghost said to protect every pirate cache.

Mull River

There is an apparition of a man with a slashed throat wearing a grey cloak, sometimes seen with a dog, who haunts the area and the Greve family. Evidently, an ancestor murdered someone in Scotland and the ghost, called the Bochdan Greve, demands retribution. A *bochdan* is a Gaelic name for hobgoblin, and these aren't the cute Hollywood goblins seen at Halloween, but a vengeful apparition which sometimes takes the form of a scarecrow.

Also, a strong witch who used to keep locals in constant fright died at the age of 118 and her witch bag is buried somewhere around here. Mary Fraser says that two men tried unsuccessfully to burn the witch bag. The bag was canvas and iron and she used it to carry items she requested from residents. Apparently, though, people didn't get much choice because she would "call upon the Devil to harm those who denied her requests."

Port Hood

Port Hood marks the beginning of special territory. This is the easternmost edge of the area that the famous Ghost Ship of Northumberland Strait sails. This ship is the second best known ghost ship from the Maritimes after the *Teazer* in Mahone Bay. From here it ranges all along the Northumberland Strait up to Baie de Chaleur. From small towns to cities, people on both sides of the Strait in three provinces have seen it. Called the Burning Ship in these parts, it appears fully ablaze, though you can still see the masts and sails through the flames. It floats across the water before suddenly plunging into the cold depths of the Northumberland Strait. Some believe they are seeing the last act of a mutiny that occurred on the ship and the mutinous souls are condemned to relive their deaths for eternity.

Antigonish County

Havre Boucher

A beautiful place of rugged views, Havre Boucher boasts one of the lesser known ghost ships of Nova Scotia. A couple of hundred years ago a British ship was attacked by pirates and set afire. The crew beat off the pirates and escaped to shore, but the ship was doomed. It is said that the spectre of the ship still sails across the bay, flames rising high, consuming the unfortunate vessel for eternity.

Also near here is the supposed resting place of pirate treasure. Known as the Black Pool, the spot is hidden by a dense growth of spruce trees. The pool is fifty feet wide and rumoured to be bottomless. Some believe the treasure is protected deep within the pool by a water system similar to that reputed to exist on Oak Island.

Dagger Woods

Dagger Woods is an area I would love to walk through on a dark and stormy night. For many years as my family and I travelled to and from Cape Breton, I would anxiously wait to see the sign announcing Dagger Woods Road, and looking down the road as we drove past I would wonder what I would find around the first curve, far into the woods. If local legends are anything to go by, then there is quite a bit in these woods to appeal to me.

Strange, awful cries come from the deep woods. This is the most commonly reported phenomenon, and may be related to an awful murder that took place here many years ago. Not much is known about the crime, but stories passed down over generations say the murderer used a pearl-handled knife and disappeared into the woods afterwards, never to be seen again. Or the terrifying cries could be related to the evil *baucan* or *bochdan* (demon or hobgoblin) of the area. This *baucan* is supposedly the most famous demon in all of Nova Scotia. He calls to you if you walk alone through the woods or along the lonely roads around here.

Meadow Green

Next to Dagger Woods is Meadow Green, and as ominous as the woods are in comparison to their name, Meadow Green is as beautiful as its name implies. But that beauty can be deceiving. Those strange, preternatural cries often reported in Dagger Woods have also been heard here.

On the old road that passes from St. Andrews to Hetherton, with Dagger Woods to its north and Meadow Green to its south, lies a haunted saltwater spring that has mystified residents for many years. Visions of a barrel hanging suspended in mid-air over the spring have been reported. Nearby, on an even older road, the phantom of an old man dressed in grey has been seen walking along the road before disappearing in an instant.

Beech Hill

The Grey Man from Meadow Green puts in an appearance here too. People have gotten a closer look at the phantom and describe his features as "horrible." Beech Hill has had strange goings-on for many years, all the way back to the last century when a peddler got lost in the woods. Tales of odd odours, rattling chains and a ghostly coffin have terrified children around here for generations. As well, the *bochdan* from Dagger Woods is said to inhabit this area from time to time.

Upper South River

There is a round hill here in the middle of a broad plain that is called Fairy Hill. To spend too much time nearby or to enter the hill is to invite all kinds of mischief from the fairies.

Lochaber

A story originates from here about one of the fairy mounds that dot the countryside. A woodcutter was on his way home to his wife and new baby when he accidentally stumbled into a mound one evening and partied with the resident leprechauns. He enjoyed himself for some time until an old man suddenly dragged him outdoors. It was then he learned the old man was his son and that the woodcutter had been gone a long time indeed.

Caledonia Mills

From this lonely yet beautiful area comes one of the more well-known stories in Nova Scotia. It concerns a fire spirit that haunted one family, the McDonalds, in 1922. In some ways this story resembles that of Esther Cox of the Great Amherst Mystery, except there is no report of these phenomena afflicting one certain person in the house.

It began with floating balls of fire being seen in the house. Then small fires were noticed around the house. During one evening alone, over thirty-eight blazes broke out inside. Later, the phenomena included ghostly footsteps, pounding on walls, and unseen hands touching a couple of investigators who were called in. The family moved out for a few months, but upon their return the fires began again. They also saw a strange animal from time to time, described as a cross between a pig and a dog and black as night.

Various explanations were advanced for the assorted phenomena, but none were entirely satisfactory. In recent years, researchers have suggested that the whole incident had been made up since it resembled a case in England that occurred just before it.

Antigonish Harbour

In the woods surrounding this town, ghosts make nocturnal wanderings, searching for we know not what. A large black dog follows travellers in the night outside of town, and it is rumoured that the Gateway to Hell exists in the hills above town. The dog is called the Devil's Hound and is sometimes accompanied by the spirit of a man who fought the demon for the soul of his brother.

North River

The North River empties into Antigonish Harbour, but at its headwaters it passes through steep hills that have an evil reputation. Mary L. Fraser describes North River Hill very poetically in her book, *Folklore of Nova Scotia*, as "steep" and "treacherous ... amid whose rough tree-clad slopes ghosts loved to wander when the night closed in."

The story goes that two men, Alex and Dan, helped a drunken friend home one night. They were accompanied by a large black dog, who refused to be chased off. Although they closed the door against the dog once they reached Alex's house, they discovered he "passed through" it. The dog spent the night going up and down the stairs, trying to reach the drunken man's room but unable to pass the door of the room where Alex's two young sisters slept. The drunken man seemed close to death that night, and Alex knelt at his bedside and prayed for him. When morning came, the man had recovered, and the dog was gone.

Malignant Cove

The cove got its name from the British warship *Malignant*, wrecked on its way to the battle on the Plains of Abraham, which finally settled the war between France and Britain for control of North America. Although there is no official record of treasure being carried by *Malignant*, popular legend has it that there must have been some gold aboard to help finance the campaign in Quebec. Lore has it the gold lies buried either in the wreck itself or along the shore. However, no sign has ever been found of it. Still, the belief is strong among the local inhabitants.

Arisaig Point

In October 1844, a millwright observed a sixty-foot black, serpentine sea monster swim by the pier. The creature was about forty feet away from the pier and appeared to be about three feet wide with small humps along its body. Both the round head and the pointed tail would rise up out of the water, then drop back under the waves.

Pictou County

Merrigomish

The last of our many stories concerning sea serpents and Nova Scotia comes from Merrigomish. Sightings have been made here of a sea monster in excess of sixty feet, dark in colour, covered in scales, with a small mane down the back of its head. Its eyes are said to reflect the light of fishermen's flashlights as it passes their boat in the night.

Melmerby Beach

In 1890, the cargo ship *Melmerby*, loaded with a shipment of timber, ran aground here northeast of New Glasgow. Only seven crew members were rescued and the wreck could be seen on the beach for many years, giving this place its name. You can still see the remains of the unfortunate ship arise out of the dark, deep waters and sometimes even hear the screams of the doomed crew.

New Glasgow

The pretty East River flows through New Glasgow, and many people enjoy boating and other activities on its blue waters. But on moonlit nights, it is said that a headless body can be seen quietly floating down the river.

In 1880, quintuplets were born in New Glasgow but lived only a short time. Because quintuplets were a rare occurrence, P.T. Barnum wanted to buy the bodies and display them in his circus. However, people feared body-snatching, so the bodies of the unfortunate babies were secretly buried in Riverside Cemetery under another name. Locals say that on certain nights if you listen closely, you can hear the spectral sounds of the babies crying out for their mother.

Pictou Harbour

In August 1803, a ship by the name of *Favourite*, out of Kirkcaldy, Scotland, unloaded passengers and freight. As soon as it lay empty it then sank for no apparent reason. This led to considerable debate about the possible causes and after a while many locals settled for a supernatural one.

Apparently, in England, before the ship sailed, one of the passengers had a run-in with a witch. The man had shot at a suspicious animal near his cows with silver bullets, suspecting it may be a witch. He hit it, but never found any body. He was never able to prove it had indeed been a witch, but an old woman in the town was suspected. She cursed him, declaring that he would never reach the New World. For this she was jailed until which time the *Favourite* reached Pictou. However, she was released early. The passenger made it to the New World safely, but the ship wasn't as lucky.

Pictou Island

There is apparently a close connection between the Phantom Ship of Northumberland Strait and Pictou Island, which lies ten miles north of Pictou. Ten miles long and two miles wide, the island has one dirt road travelling its length with another road bisecting it at the western end. The ghostly figure of a woman in white, with an unearthly wind blowing her long hair out behind her, walks down the main road on the eastern side of the island to a point offshore where a bright, burning light awaits her. When the spectre reaches the light, it changes into the now famous sailing ship, all aglow in flames. Then the ship suddenly sinks, and everything is dark and quiet again.

Six Mile Brook

One of my favourite types of stories has to do with spectres that appear along roads, bridges or railway tracks. There is something hauntingly romantic and tragic about the thought of a spirit endlessly trying to make it home but never managing it. From time to time on a back road near Six Mile Bridge appears an elderly lady with a shawl on her head and dressed in nineteenth-century clothes. Any driver who stops to offer assistance is not surprised to discover she has vanished, since this short play has been re-enacted many times.

Scotsburn

This phantom is more often heard than seen, at least by humans. Legend has it the Black Dog haunts this area and is most often seen and heard by other dogs, though rarely a human will catch a glimpse of the spectre. A little easier to see is the phantom light that follows hunters through the woods, especially near an old dam.

Epilogue

Not everyone is as fortunate as I am to have had a family fascinated by stories of the mysterious, an Uncle Al to pass on that fascination, and the opportunity to eavesdrop as a youngster to hear spine-tingling tales first-hand. However, as Nova Scotians, we have a wealth of ghost stories, by volume and by the sheer variety of our cultural heritage. Storytelling is a vibrant pastime here, where we keep the beliefs of our ancestors alive by relating traditional stories. Ghost stories continue to thrill us with their mystery and their ability to terrify us. What better way to spend a foggy or stormy evening in Nova Scotia than to gather your friends and family around you and tell some tales of spooks and spectres?

We love to be scared – and it is fun to believe. The poster for the 1978 movie *Dawn of the Dead* read, "When there's no more room in HELL, the dead will walk the EARTH." Not too many people could read that and not shiver – some, delightedly – at the thought. The dead are dead, and we wish for them to remain so. Although we would wish them back to life *as they were*, we would not like to meet them in their present state. They remind us of our own mortality, what we will all become one day, and we want that fact hidden away from us in hospitals and funeral homes.

But we enjoy *pretending* we want to meet the dead, or that if we did come across a horrifying spectre, we would live to tell the tale. That is why traditional ghost stories and Hollywood movies do so well. We get to walk away from death, to spurn it as we leave the theatre, close the book, or turn the channel. We control death. And in our religious beliefs, we can be comforted by the thought that we shall meet old friends and loved ones as they are "risen up on the last day."

Before my Uncle Al died, my mother was visiting him at River Bourgeois and asked him if he went upstairs a lot. Uncle Al, a World War Two veteran and a member of the RCAF, was a big, strapping man, not the sort to be easily frightened or intimidated. But he responded to my mother's question by saying he rarely ventured upstairs, "for there are too many ghosts up there." Which leads to my mother's story.

When she was twelve years old, she was sleeping in the larger bedroom with my Aunt Phyllis. One night my mother woke up and watched a blue ball of light come into the room and float around until it reached the foot of her bed. At this point, my mother quite understandably hid under the covers, and the blue light vanished. It could have been a case of ball lightning, or it could have been a ghostly spirit revisiting its old home, a classic example of a *feu follet*, the jack o'lantern. Many people have died in this house, and perhaps some of them return.

Such stories of the supernatural often seem incredible or even impossible – and for some, perhaps there is a logical, scientific explanation – but there are clearly too many such examples to simply ignore, as the tales of ghosts, ghost ships, mysterious fire, Grey Ladies, and other ghoulish manifestations in this book bear out.

Such stories suggest the possibility that we just don't know about other planes of existence, and they often speak to our need to know the dead are not lost to us – although we might prefer our encounters with them to spare us any gory sights. Many people, like my mother, have had some paranormal experience, and countless others are like my Uncle Al; they *know* something lurks in the dark above the stairs.

If you know of any stories that will strike fear into the most stalwart heart and which could be included in future editions, or if you have something you wish to have investigated, please contact me at bookresearch@eastlink.ca. I am always interested in any story concerning the paranormal anywhere in the country.

Glossary of Terms

Angels: Bodiless, immortal spirits, limited in knowledge and power, and created by God to watch over and assist humans. There are various types of angels: seraphim, cherubim, thrones, dominions, virtues, powers, principalities, archangels, and angels. Most do not have any function on earth and do not appear as human or cherubs.

Anomalistic Psychology: The psychological study of phenomena that is considered unconventional and in possible contradiction of generally held beliefs. Anomalistic psychologists seek to understand and explain these phenomena through conventional theories.

Apparition: A vision of a person or place that is not actually there. Often called ghosts, apparitions differ from ghosts in that they are sentient and seek to interact with the living. Apparitions are divided into four types: Crisis Apparitions – the appearance of a spirit within twelve hours of death; Postmortem Apparitions – the appearance of a spirit after twelve hours of death has elapsed. These are the most common manifestations of apparitions; Experimental Apparitions – the purposeful appearance of live persons to each other; Residual Apparitions –

a catch-all category that includes religious appearances such as the Virgin Mary, as well as appearances of live people.

Banshee: A female Irish ghost that only appears to herald an upcoming death. The spirits were said to wail and moan so loudly that any loud screaming sound is compared to a banshee.

Bocan: A spirit in Gaelic mythology resembling the English Goblin. It is a terrifying apparition that haunts the glens of Scotland and Cape Breton. The Bocan was the inspiration for popular tales of the bogeyman.

Bochda, Bochdan, Bochdain, Bhochdain, Bochdainn: Originally denoting fieldworkers or soothsayers, the term now refers to a terrifying creature in Atlantic Canadian mythology. The *bochdan* is a revenge-seeking creature of the land that is the result of a wrongful death. It can be seen in many forms and often has its death-wounds visible. Unlike many other spirits, ***bochdans*** can cross water, and are known to harass their murderers until justice is done.

Cryptozoology: The scientific search for "hidden animals," commonly called Cryptids. These animals are those thought to be extinct or not yet classified by zoology. The most common cryptids being sought by researchers are Sasquatch (Bigfoot), the Yeti, Loch Ness Monster, and lesser lake and sea monsters.

Curses: The alleged calling upon of supernatural forces to do harm to a person. An integral part of the Witchcraft craze of the 1400s to 1700s.

Fairies: Mythical beings that are said to exist in a middle ground between angels and humans. They appeared as petite people with a wry sense of humour and were easily crossed. They were said to steal children and replace them with Changelings, beings that looked like the replaced children, but were not. They had their own realm and could kidnap those who were foolish enough to come close. Many small hills or barrows were said to be entrances to their realms. Fairies were accomplished musicians, especially with the fiddle.

Fairy Mounds: This phrase originates in ancient Ireland and refers to the belief that Fairies used to build forts to protect their realm. Probably originated when older abandoned fortifications or dwellings from earlier settlers were found by new settlers hundreds of years later.

Foxfire: Luminous light phenomenon most often observed at night and caused by decaying wood products. Often assumed to be of a paranormal nature.

Ghost: See Apparition

Ghost Investigation: A formal, controlled research project of a site thought to be haunted. Various techniques and equipment are used by university or other official organizations to scientifically determine the nature and behaviour of ghosts. There is special attention to controlling the area so as to eliminate other more mundane explanations for any anomalous findings.

Ghost Hunt: An informal, usually for fun adventure to a place that is thought to be haunted. Although equipment is sometimes used to gain scientific readings, the informality or amateurishness of the attempt makes useful conclusions impossible.

Ghost Hunter: A person who seeks to understand the nature of ghosts and hauntings, either informally or scientifically.

Ghostbuster: A person who claims to be able to remove a ghost or stop a haunting. It is a derogatory term coined in the 1980s with the *Ghostbuster* movies.

Goblin, Hobgoblin, Brownie, Gnome: A goblin is a legendary evil or mischievous creature, described as grotesquely evil. Goblins have conflicting abilities, temperaments and appearances depending on the story and country of origin. Hobgoblin is a term used to describe a friendly but troublesome creature. Brownies and gnomes are most commonly associated with hobgoblins and goblins.

Grey Lady: A popular apparition in Nova Scotia, particularly along the Eastern Shore, though the most famous one is found in Annapolis County near Port Royal. No one is sure why some female apparitions appear as white and others as grey, but popular belief is that Grey Ladies are beset by deep sadness and are doomed to wander the earth, lost in their grief.

Hairy Bipeds: A category of unknown humanoids separate from Sasquatch (Bigfoot) and the Yeti. These humanoids resemble the Pacific Northwest Sasquatch, yet they have been reported in every state and province of the U.S. and Canada. They also have characteristics that differ from Sasquatch – for example, three toes – and some are reported able to disappear. Whereas Sasquatch conforms to general physical laws for a primate (either an ape-like human or a human-like ape), these creatures are not zoologically possible. It is for these reasons that researchers believe these creatures are not real and are a product of the same hallucinatory process that accounts for some UFO reports.

Lake Monsters: Varied and mysterious group of creatures said to inhabit fresh water lakes across the world in the Northern Hemisphere. The most famous of all lake monsters is the Loch Ness Monster in Scotland, which is popularly believed to be that of an extinct plesiosaur or Zeuglodon. However, Scotland has other lochs with alleged monsters in them as do Norway, Sweden, Finland, and Canada. Related to these are the serpentine creatures off both coasts of North America and around the British Isles. The most famous is Cadborosaurus, which is reported off the British Columbia coast. It is difficult to determine whether most reports of these creatures are folklore, known but misidentified animals, or unknown or formerly extinct animals.

Omen: A happening that is believed to foretell the future. Omens can be either good or bad.

Paracryptozoology: A fringe subset of cryptozoology in which members believe that some mysterious creatures such as Sasquatch and the Loch Ness Monster are actually paranormal manifestations. This view is dismissed by all but a few researchers such as John Keel and Loren Coleman.

Paranormal: Literally, "beside the normal." Wide-ranging and unrelated events that violate normal conventions of time and space, and cause and effect.

Parapsychology: "Beside psychology." The scientific investigation of Extrasensory Perception (ESP), Psychokinesis (PK) and, to a lesser degree, ghosts. It grew out of the psychical research efforts of the 1800s and uses stringent research methods to investigate and test theories related to its mandate.

Phantom Hitchhiker: A usually spurious tale (Urban Legend) that may have had some truth originally. There is some evidence that the first Phantom Hitchhiker tale came out of Arkansas in 1929 and concerned a woman that appeared to drivers on a bridge, requesting to be taken to her home. Upon arrival at said home, she would be mysteriously missing from the back seat. The most famous PH is Resurrection Mary out of Chicago, Illinois. She appears outside of Resurrection Cemetery and courteously accepts a drive home, only to vanish before they reach it.

Poltergeist: From the German, meaning "noisy spirit." Although classified as a form of ghost, it is commonly believed to be a form of unconscious psychokinesis, usually exhibited by a female teenager. There are thought to be five levels of poltergeist activity, ranging from mild to extremely dangerous. However, the first three levels are indistinguishable from a "normal" haunting, and levels four and five have never been proven factual. The possibility exists that poltergeists are in fact exaggerated or false reports of hauntings.

Psychokinesis: Also denoted as PK, psychokinesis is the alleged ability of a person to influence the environment with their mind, rather than conventional means.

Wicca (Witchcraft): An ancient earth religion, demonized by the Catholic Church and popularly known as Witchcraft. One of the many pagan religions that existed prior to the advent of Christianity, Wicca survived a long period of persecution and thrives to this day. Contrary to popular belief, Wicca (and Witchcraft) did not practice Devil Worship, for the Devil is a being Wiccan practitioners do not recognize.

Will-O'-The-Wisp: A will-o'-the-wisp, or *ignis fatuus* (meaning foolish fire), is a ghostly light sometimes seen at night or over bogs, swamps, and marshes. It resembles a flickering lamp and is often mistaken for the manifestation of a ghost in torment.

Women in White: Referred to as Wandering Women in White by Helen Creighton, they are the most common female apparition found in Nova Scotia. Thought to be the spirits of women who have died before they have completed some task, or are earthbound by grief or loss.

Wraith: An older term for Crisis Apparition.

Bibliography

Armet, Chad. *The Historical Bigfoot: Early Reports of Wild Men, Hairy Giants, and Wandering Gorillas in North America*. Landisville, Pennsylvania: Coachwhip Publications, 2006.

Baigent, Michael, Richard Leigh, and Henry Lincoln. *The Holy Blood and the Holy Grail*. London: Jonathan Cape, 1982.

Bauchman, Rosemary. *The Best of Helen Creighton*. Hantsport, Nova Scotia: Lancelot Press, 1988.

Bauchman, Rosemary. *Love is Stranger than Death*. Hantsport, Nova Scotia: Lancelot Press, 1985.

Bauchman, Rosemary. *Mysteries and Marvels*. Hantsport, Nova Scotia: Lancelot Press, 1991.

Borrett, William C. *Down East: Another Cargo of Tales Told Under the Old Town Clock*. Halifax, Nova Scotia: The Imperial Publishing Co. Ltd., 1945.

Borrett, William C. *Down to the Sea Again with Tales Told Under the Old Town Clock*. Halifax, N.S.: The Imperial Publishing Co. Ltd., 1947.

Borrett, Willam C. *East Coast Port and Other Tales Told Under the Old Town Clock.* Halifax, N.S.: The Imperial Publishing Co. Ltd., 1946.

Borrett, William C. *Tales Told Under the Old Town Clock.* Halifax, Nova Scotia: The Imperial Publishing Co. Ltd., 1942.

Bradley, Michael. *Holy Grail Across the Atlantic: The Secret History of Canadian Discovery and Exploration.* Willowdale, Ontario: Hounslow Press, 1988.

Broadbent, Terry, Ed. *Cries at Kinsac Corner and Other Legends.* Bedford, Nova Scotia: Self-published, date unknown.

Campbell, Lyall. *Sable Island: Fatal and Fertile Crescent.* Hantsport, Nova Scotia: Lancelot Press, 1990.

Caplan, Ronald, Ed. *Another Night: Cape Breton Stories True & Short & Tall.* Wreck Cove, Nova Scotia: Breton Books, 1995.

Caplan, Ronald. *Cape Breton Book of the Night: Tales of Tenderness and Terror.* Wreck Cove, Nova Scotia: Breton Books, 1991.

Chisholm, Archie Neil, Brian Sutcliffe and Ronald Caplan, Eds. *"As True As I'm Sitting Here."* Wreck Cove, Nova Scotia: Breton Books, 2000.

Columbo, John Robert. *Mysterious Canada: Strange Sights, Extraordinary Events, and Peculiar Places.* Toronto: Doubleday, 1988.

Creighton, Helen. *Bluenose Ghosts.* Toronto: McGraw-Hill Ryerson Ltd., 1957.

Creighton, Helen. *Bluenose Magic.* Hantsport, Nova Scotia: Lancelot Press, 1968.

Creighton, Helen. *Folklore of Lunenburg County, Nova Scotia.* Toronto: McGraw-Hill, Ryerson Ltd., 1950.

Crooker, William S. *Oak Island Gold.* Halifax, Nova Scotia: Nimbus Publishing Ltd., 1993.

Crooker, William S. *The Oak Island Quest.* Hantsport, Nova Scotia: Lancelot Press, 1978.

Crooker, William S. *Tracking Treasure: In Search of East Coast Bounty.* Halifax, Nova Scotia: Nimbus Publishing, 1998.

Crowell, Bill. *Atlantic Treasure Troves.* Hantsport, Nova Scotia: Lancelot Press, 1985.

Cuthbertson, Brian. *The Halifax Citadel.* Halifax, Nova Scotia: Formac Publishing Co. Ltd., 2001.

Evans, Millie and Eric Mullen. *Oak Island, Nova Scotia: The World's Greatest Treasure Hunt.* Halifax, Nova Scotia: Four East Publications Ltd., 1984.

Fanthorpe, Lionel and Patricia. *The Oak Island Mystery: The Secret of the World's Greatest Treasure Hunt.* Toronto: Hounslow Press, 1994.

Finnan, Mark. *Oak Island Secrets.* Halifax, Nova Scotia: Formac Publishing, 1995.

Finucane, R.C. *Ghosts: Appearances of the Dead & Cultural Transformation.* Amherst, New York: Prometheus Books, 1996.

Fowke, Edith and Carole H. Carpenter. *Explorations in Canadian Folklore.* Toronto: McClelland & Stewart, 1985.

Fowke, Edith. *Forklore of Canada.* Toronto: McClelland & Stewart, 1976.

Fraser, Mary L. *Folklore of Nova Scotia.* Antigonish, Nova Scotia: Formac Ltd., No date.

Furneaux, Rupert. *Money Pit: Mystery of Oak Island.* Toronto: Totem Books, 1972.

Gesner, Claribel. *Cape Breton Vignettes.* Hantsport, Nova Scotia: Lancelot Press, 1974.

Government of Canada. Canadian Historic Sites #9. Department of Indian and Northern Affairs, Ottawa, 1975.

Halpert, Herbert, Ed. *A Folklore Sampler From the Maritimes.* St. John's, Newfoundland: Memorial University of Newfoundland, 1982.

Hand, Chris M. *The Seige of Fort Beausejour, 1755.* Fredericton, New Brunswick: Goose Lane Editions and The New Brunswick Military Heritage Project, 2004.

Harris, Graham, and Les MacPhie. *Oak Island and its Lost Treasure.* 2nd Edition. Halifax, Nova Scotia: Formac Publishing Co. Ltd., 2005.

Haverstock, George. *Discover McNab's Island.* Halifax, Nova Scota: Friends of McNab's Island Society, 1995.

Henniger, Ted. *Scotian Spooks: Mystery and Violence.* Hantsport, Nova Scotia: Lancelot Press, 1978.

Jessome, Bill. *Maritime Mysteries and the Ghosts Who Surround Us.* Halifax, Nova Scotia: Nimbus Publishing, 1999.

Jessome, Bill. *More Maritime Mysteries.* Halifax, Nova Scotia: Nimbus Publishing, 2001.

Jessome, Bill. *The Stories That Haunt Us.* Halifax, Nova Scotia: Nimbus Publishing, 2004.

LeVert, Suzanne. *Let's Discover Canada: Nova Scotia.* New York: Chelsea House Publishing, 1992.

Marshall, Dianne. *George's Island: The Keep of Halifax Harbour.* Halifax, Nova Scotia: Nimbus Publishing, 2003.

Mitcham, Allison. *Offshore Islands of Nova Scotia and New Brunswick.* Hantsport, Nova Scotia: Lancelot Press, 1992.

Mooney Jr, Fraser. *Jerome: Solving the Mystery of Nova Scotia's Silent Castaway.* Halifax, Nova Scotia: Nimbus Publishing, 2008.

Mosher, Edith. *Haunted: Tales of the Unexplained.* Hantsport, Nova Scotia: Lancelot Press, 1982.

Mosher, Edith. *The Sea and the Supernatural.* Hantsport, Nova Scotia: Lancelot Press, 1991.

Norris, Laurie Glenn. *Cumberland County: Facts and Folklore.* Halifax, Nova Scotia: Nimbus Publishing, 2009.

Oickle, Vernon. *Canada's Haunted Coast: True Ghost Stories of the Maritimes.* Edmonton, Alberta: Ghost House Books (Lone Pine Publishing), 2008.

Oickle, Vernon. *Ghost Stories of the Maritimes.* Edmonton, Alberta: Lone Pine Publishing, 2001.

Oickle, Vernon. *Ghost Stories of the Maritimes, Volume 2.* Edmonton, Alberta: Lone Pine Publishing, 2001

Raddall, Thomas. *Footsteps on Old Floors.* Lawrencetown Beach, Nova Scotia: Pottersfield Press, 1992.

Samson, David Lloyd. *Island of Ghosts: Folklore and Strange Tales of the Supernatural from Cape Breton.* Hantsport, Nova Scotia: Lancelot Press, 1992.

Sherwood, Roland. *The Bride's Ship and Other Tales of the Unusual.* Hantsport, Nova Scotia: Lancelot Press, 1990.

Sherwood, Roland. *Legends, Oddities, and Facts of the Maritime Provinces.* Hantsport, Nova Scotia: Lancelot Press, 1984.

Sherwood, Roland. *Maritime Mysteries.* Hantsport, Nova Scotia: Lancelot Press, 1976.

Sherwood, Roland. *The Phantom Ship of Northumberland Strait and Other Mysteries of the Sea.* Hantsport, Nova Scotia: Lancelot Press, 1975.

Sherwood, Roland. *Sagas of the Land and Sea.* Hantsport, Nova Scotia: Lancelot Press, 1990.

Snow, Edward Rowe. *Ghosts, Gales and Gold.* New York: Dodd, Mead & Co, 1972.

Spice, Stanley T. *Mary Celeste.* Hantsport, Nova Scotia: Lancelot Press, 1993.

Sutcliffe, Brian, Ed. *Stories I've Been Told: The Maritime Storytellers of CBC's Weekend Mornings.* Lawrencetown Beach, Nova Scotia: Potterfield Press, 1999.

Trueman, Stuart. *Tall Tales and True Tales from Down East.* Toronto: McClelland & Stewart, 1979.

Underwood, Jay. Ghost Tracks. *Surprising Stories of the Supernatural on Rails.* Montreal: Railfare DC Books, 2009.

Vernon, Steve. *Halifax Haunts: Exploring the City's Spookiest Places.* Halifax, Nova Scotia: Nimbus Publishing, 2009.

Vernon, Steve. *Haunted Harbours: Ghost Stories from old Nova Scotia.* Halifax, Nova Scotia: Nimbus Publishing, 2006.

Watson, Julie. *Ghost Stories and Legends of Prince Edward Island.* Toronto: Hounslow Press, 1988.

Watts, Heather and Michele Raymond. *Halifax's Northwest Arm: An Illustrated History.* Halifax, Nova Scotia: Formac Publishing Co. Ltd., 2003.

Young, George. *Ancient Peoples and Modern Ghosts.* Queensland, Nova Scotia: George Young, 1987.

Young, George. *Ghosts in Nova Scotia.* Queensland, Nova Scotia: George Young, 1977.

Also Available From Pottersfield Press

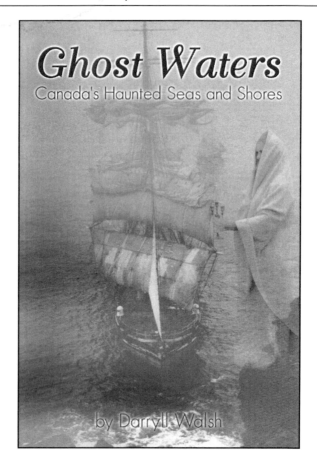

Ghost Waters
Canada's Haunted Seas and Shores
by Darryll Walsh
ISBN 10: 1-895900-49-2
ISBN 13: 978-1-895900-49-1
$16.95

Seventy-two eerie, supernatural mysteries from across Canada
that occurred at sea, on rivers, on lakes or along the shorelines.